AF442534

VIETNAMESE AND INDIAN COOKBOOK

2 Books In 1: Learn How To Cook At Home Tasty And Spicy Food From Vietnam And India

Maki Blanc

VIETNAMESE
COOKBOOK

70 Easy Recipes for Asian Foods from Vietnam.

Maki Blanc

© **Copyright 2021 by Maki Blanc - All rights reserved.**

This document is geared towards providing exact and reliable information in regard to the topic and issue covered. The publication is sold with the idea that the publisher is not required to render accounting, officially permitted, or otherwise, qualified services. If advice is necessary, legal or professional, a practiced individual in the profession should be ordered.

From a Declaration of Principles which was accepted and approved equally by a Committee of the American Bar Association and a Committee of Publishers and Associations.

In no way is it legal to reproduce, duplicate, or transmit any part of this document in either electronic means or in printed format. Recording of this publication is strictly prohibited and any storage of this document is not allowed unless with written permission from the publisher. All rights reserved.

The information provided herein is stated to be truthful and consistent, in that any liability, in terms of inattention or otherwise, by any usage or abuse of any policies, processes, or directions contained within is the solitary and utter responsibility of the recipient reader. Under no circumstances will any legal responsibility or blame be held against the publisher for any reparation, damages, or monetary loss due to the information herein, either directly or indirectly.

Respective authors own all copyrights not held by the publisher.

The information herein is offered for informational purposes solely and is universal as so. The presentation of the information is without contract or any type of guarantee assurance.

The trademarks that are used are without any consent, and the publication of the trademark is without permission or backing by the trademark owner. All trademarks and brands within this book are for clarifying purposes only and are owned by the owners themselves, not affiliated with this document.

Contents

Introduction

Although culinary art of Asian countries has long been globally admired for numerous delicious and elaborately-ornamented dishes, Vietnamese cuisine still wins the heart of numerous foodies nationally and internationally due to its fresh ingredients, refreshing taste and exquisite presentation.

Culinary culture is normally shaped by the way a society lives. The Vietnamese culture promotes the addition of various new flavors into their food. No explorers have yet succeeded in resisting the amazing flavors of Vietnamese dishes.

The food of the north is intensely inspired by China with its sautés and noodle-based soups. As you move to the south, there are more flavors of Thailand and Cambodia in the Vietnamese food. The heat and humidity in the south region of Vietnam is favorable for rice paddies, coconut forests, jackfruit trees, and spice gardens. The food in southern Vietnam is usually more flavorful i.e. better flavors for pho, more palm sugar utilized in exquisite dishes, and those well-known taffy-like coconut confectioners made with the help of coconut cream.

In this book, you will learn various different recipes originated from Vietnam. The recipe section will include breakfast, lunch, dinner, snacks, and sweet dishes. All these recipes are detailed with easy to follow instructions and detailed ingredients that help you out in cooking by these at home. So, start reading this amazing book now.

Chapter 1: The World of Vietnamese Breakfast Recipes

The morning meal in Vietnam is viewed as the main feast of the day. In various societies, they start the day with their own novel dishes. Following are the recipes listed below:

1.1 Vietnamese Fried Egg Recipe

Preparation Time: 30 minutes
Cooking Time: 10 minutes
Serving: 4

Ingredients:

- Spring onions, four
- Rice noodles, two cups
- Pepper to taste
- Butter, as required
- Salt to taste
- Baby plum tomatoes, four
- Eggs, four
- Cilantro, half cup

Instructions:

1. Boil the rice noodles according to the instructions on the package.
2. Once cooked, drain the noodles.
3. Put the butter in a pan.
4. Add the spring onions and chili into the small pan.
5. Cook for a couple of minutes until softened.

6. Whisk the milk and eggs in a bowl.
7. Add the eggs to the pan.
8. Fry the eggs.
9. Add the tomatoes and coriander leaves on top.
10. Once cooked, dish it out.
11. Add the eggs on top of the noodles.
12. The dish is ready to be served.

1.2 Vietnamese Breakfast Burgers Recipe

Preparation Time: 20 minutes
Cooking Time: 20 minutes
Serving: 4

Ingredients:

- Jalapenos, as required
- Chicken filet, four
- Mayonnaise, half cup
- Carrots, two
- Butter, two tablespoon
- Eggs, eight
- Burger buns, four
- Fish sauce, as required
- Cucumber, two
- Salt and pepper, to taste
- Cooking oil, as required

Instructions:

1. Take a large bowl.
2. Add the dry ingredients in a bowl.
3. Mix all the ingredients well.
4. Cook the chicken filet in a pan full of oil.

5. Dish out the chicken when it turns golden brown from both sides.
6. Toast the buns by adding a little butter on both sides.
7. Assemble the burgers.
8. Add all the ingredients one by one on top of the bun.
9. You can serve the burgers with any preferred sauce.
10. The dish is ready to be served.

1.3 Vietnamese Steamed Rice Rolls with Pork Recipe

Preparation Time: 30 minutes
Cooking Time: 15 minutes
Serving: 4

Ingredients:

- Thin soy sauce, one tablespoon
- Pepper powder, half tablespoon
- Sugar, one tablespoon
- Garlic powder, one tablespoon
- Fresh shallot, half tablespoon
- Milk, one cup
- Vegetable oil, one tablespoon
- Steamed rice, one cup
- Whole wheat flour, half cup
- Salt, to taste
- Water, to knead
- Pulled pork, one cup
- Yeast, two teaspoon

Instructions:

1. Take a bowl and add the steamed rice into it.
2. Then add the yeast and sugar into it.
3. Add lukewarm water in it.
4. Set aside for half hour.
5. Add the whole wheat flour into it.
6. Then add the salt and some water in it.
7. Then combine the ingredients to form a soft dough.
8. Meanwhile, mix the pulled pork and rest of the filling ingredients
9. Make round forms of dough with the help of the oil.
10. Add the mixture in middle of the dough and place on a tray.
11. Seam the rolls for fifteen minutes.
12. Your dish is ready to be served.

1.4 Vietnamese Crepes Recipe

Preparation Time: 10 minutes
Cooking Time: 15 minutes
Serving: 2

Ingredients:

- Almond milk, one cup
- Cilantro as required
- Almond oil, two tablespoon
- Tapioca flour, half cup
- Almond flour, half cup
- Eggs, three
- Arrowroot starch, half teaspoon

Instructions:

1. Mix in both the flours in a bowl.
2. Mix the ingredients carefully.
3. Add the mixture in small quantities in a pan.
4. Let the crepes turn golden on both sides.
5. Add a little cilantro on top of your crepes.
6. You can add fresh fruits as well on the top.
7. You can garnish the crepes with any other ingredient that you prefer.
8. Your dish is ready to be served.

1.5 Vietnamese Breakfast Bowl Recipe

Preparation Time: 10 minutes
Cooking Time: 20 minutes
Serving: 4

Ingredients:

- Coconut milk, half cup
- Wild blueberries, one cup
- Coconut oil, one tablespoon
- Sliced almonds, two tablespoon
- Milk, two cups
- Almond extract, one teaspoon
- Dry rolled oats, one cup
- Coconut cream, one cup

Instructions:
1. Combine all the ingredients together in a bowl.
2. Pour the mixture into a baking dish coated with coconut oil.
3. Add the one cup of frozen wild blueberries on top.
4. Sprinkle the sliced almonds on top.
5. Set the dishes on a flat sheet pan.

6. Bake for twenty-five minutes in a preheated oven.
7. When cooked, dish out and add fresh berries on top.
8. Your dish is ready to be served.

1.6 Vietnamese Happy Pancakes Recipe

Preparation Time: 20 minutes
Cooking Time: 20 minutes
Serving: 4

Ingredients:

- Sliced apples, one cup
- Sugar, four tablespoon
- Salt, as required
- Cilantro as required
- Sesame oil, two tablespoon
- Tapioca flour, half cup
- Almond flour, half cup
- Sliced peaches, one cup
- Coconut cream, a quarter cup
- Coconut milk, one cup

Instructions:

1. Mix in both the flours in a bowl.
2. Add the sliced peaches and apples into the bowl.
3. Add in the sugar and rest of the ingredients.
4. Mix the ingredients carefully.
5. Grease a pan with sesame oil.
6. Add the mixture in small quantities in a pan.
7. Let the pancakes turn golden on both sides.
8. Add a little cilantro on top of the pancakes.

9. You can garnish the pancakes with any other topping that you prefer.
10.   Your dish is ready to be served.

1.7 Vietnamese Breakfast Pastries Recipe

Preparation Time: 2 hours
Cooking Time: 10 minutes
Serving: 4

Ingredients:

- Salt, to taste
- Pepper, to taste
- Milk, two cups
- White sugar, half cup
- Salt, one teaspoon
- Eggs, two
- Cooked ground pork, one cup
- Fish sauce, one teaspoon
- Oyster sauce, one teaspoon
- All-purpose flour, two cups
- Butter, one cup
- Dry yeast, one cup

Instructions:
1. Take a medium bowl and add the butter in it.
2. Add the flour and mix well.
3. Then refrigerate it.
4. Take a large bowl and add the yeast into it.

5. Add the sugar, salt and milk.
6. Mix the warm milk mixture with the flour and the yeast.
7. Add the eggs, the lemon extract and the almond extract together.
8. Then knead it in the flour until the dough is formed.
9. Place butter on dough and fold it.
10. Make pastries from the dough roll.
11. Take a small bowl.
12. Add the pork, salt, pepper and the sauces.
13. Add the pork mixture in the pastry dough.
14. Bake them for ten minutes.
15. The pastry is ready to be served.

1.8 Vietnamese Scrambled Eggs with Fish Sauce Recipe

Preparation Time: 30 minutes
Cooking Time: 10 minutes
Serving: 4

Ingredients:

- Onions, one
- Chopped garlic, one teaspoon
- Butter, two tablespoon
- Fish sauce, half cup
- Mixed vegetables, half pound
- Salt, to taste
- Black pepper, to taste
- Chopped fresh chives, as required
- Eggs, twelve

Instructions:

1. Take a large pan.
2. Add the butter and let it meltdown.
3. Add in the chopped onion.
4. Cook the onion until soft.
5. Add in the garlic.
6. Mix the onions and garlic for two minutes and add in the mixed vegetables.
7. Add the eggs and let them cook.
8. Scramble the mixture.
9. Add in the salt and pepper.
10. Add in the fish sauce in the end.
11. When the eggs are done, dish them out.
12. Add the fresh chopped chives on top.
13. Your dish is ready to be served.

1.9 Vietnamese Steak and Eggs Recipe

Preparation Time: 10 minutes
Cooking Time: 20 minutes
Serving: 4

Ingredients:

- Powdered garlic, half teaspoon
- Eggs, four
- Steak meat, half pound
- Turmeric, half teaspoon
- Mixed vegetables, one cup
- Sea salt, to taste
- Coconut oil, two tablespoon
- Mixed spice, half teaspoon
- Onion, one
- Fish sauce, one tablespoon

- Oyster sauce, two tablespoon
- Dried thyme, half teaspoon
- Powdered ginger, half teaspoon

Instructions:
1. Heat the coconut oil in a pan.
2. Add the steak meat.
3. Dish out the meat when done and slice it up.
4. Add the mixed vegetables and spices.
5. Once they turn soft, add in the eggs as well.
6. Add the spices and cook it for five to ten minutes or until the eggs are cooked.
7. Add in the sliced steaks.
8. Mix the dish well and cook for five minutes.
9. Your dish is ready to be served.

1.10 Vietnamese Scrambled Eggs with Pork Mince Recipe

Preparation Time: 30 minutes
Cooking Time: 10 minutes
Serving: 4

Ingredients:

- Onions, one
- Chopped garlic, one teaspoon

- Butter, two tablespoon
- Fish sauce, half cup
- Oyster sauce, half tablespoon
- Mixed spices, one tablespoon
- Pork mince, half pound
- Salt, to taste
- Black pepper, to taste
- Chopped fresh chives, as required
- Eggs, twelve

Instructions:
1. Take a large pan.
2. Add the butter and let it meltdown.
3. Add in the chopped onion.
4. Cook the onion until soft.
5. Add in the garlic.
6. Mix the onions and garlic for two minutes and add in the minced pork.
7. Add the eggs and let it cook.
8. Scramble the mixture.
9. Add in the salt, mixed spice and pepper.
10. Add in the fish sauce and the oyster sauce in the end.
11. When the eggs are done dish them out.
12. Add the fresh chopped chives on top.
13. Your dish is ready to be served.

1.11 Vietnamese Breakfast Egg Rolls Recipe

Preparation Time: 15 minutes
Cooking Time: 25 minutes
Serving: 4

Ingredients:

- Cooked eggs, three
- Canola oil, one cup
- Minced garlic, two tablespoon
- Chopped red onion, one cup
- Coconut milk, one cup
- Lime juice, two tablespoon
- Water, as required
- Wonton wrappers, as required
- Cilantro leaves, as required
- Salt, a pinch

Instructions:
1. Take a bowl.
2. Add the eggs and garlic powder.
3. Add more oil into it and add all the ingredients.
4. Add the chopped red onions, coconut milk and water as required.
5. Add the lime juice and cilantro leaves into it.
6. Add the salt and pepper as required.
7. Add the ingredients into the wrappers and roll them.
8. Serve the rolls with soy sauce.
9. Your dish is ready to be served.

1.12 Vietnamese Tofu Pancakes Recipe

Preparation Time: 20 minutes
Cooking Time: 20 minutes
Serving: 4

Ingredients:

- Ground garlic, half teaspoon
- Salt, as required
- Black pepper, two
- Ground pepper, as required
- Red onion, one
- Cilantro as required
- Sesame oil, two tablespoon
- Tapioca flour, half cup
- Almond flour, half cup
- Shredded tofu, one cup
- Coconut milk, one cup
- Fish sauce, half teaspoon
- Ground ginger, half teaspoon

Instructions:
1. Mix in both the flours in a bowl.
2. Add the chopped red onions.
3. Add the shredded tofu into the bowl.
4. Add in the spices, black pepper, fish sauce and cilantro.
5. Mix the ingredients carefully.
6. Grease a pan with sesame oil.
7. Add the mixture in small quantities in a pan.
8. Let the pancakes turn golden on both sides.
9. Add a little cilantro on top of your pancakes.
10. Your dish is ready to be served.

Chapter 2: The World of Vietnamese Lunch Recipes

Large numbers of the most famous Vietnamese dishes can be made very easily at home. Following are some classic Vietnamese recipes that are rich in healthy nutrients and you can easily make them with the detailed instructions list in each recipe:

2.1 Vietnamese Prawn and Papaya Salad Recipe

Preparation Time: 10 minutes
Cooking Time: 30 minutes
Serving: 2

Ingredients:

- Prawn pieces, half pound
- Maple syrup, one teaspoon
- Ground ginger, a quarter teaspoon
- Papaya, two
- Mixed nuts, two tablespoon
- Pepper, as required
- Cilantro, half cup
- Salt, a quarter teaspoon
- Soy sauce, as required
- Mint leaves, half cup
- Salad dressing, half cup

Instructions:

1. Peel the papaya and then cut into large pieces.

2. Boil the prawn pieces, drain them and slice them into a bowl.
3. Mix all the ingredients along with the prawns and papaya.
4. In a bowl, add the salad dressing and beat it well.
5. Drizzle the dressing on top of the prawns and papaya mixture.
6. Your dish is ready to be served.

2.2 Vietnamese Chicken Salad Recipes

Preparation Time: 10 minutes
Cooking Time: 30 minutes
Serving: 2

Ingredients:

- Chicken pieces, half pound
- Maple syrup, one teaspoon
- Ground ginger, a quarter teaspoon
- Mixed fruit, half cup
- Mixed nuts, two tablespoon
- Pepper, as required
- Cilantro, half cup
- Salt, a quarter teaspoon
- Soy sauce, as required
- Mint leaves, half cup
- Salad dressing, half cup

Instructions:

1. Peel the fruits and then cut them into large pieces.
2. Boil the chicken pieces, drain them and slice them into a bowl.
3. Mix all the ingredients along with the chicken and fruits.
4. In a bowl, add the salad dressing and beat it well.
5. Drizzle the dressing on top of the chicken and fruit mixture.
6. Your dish is ready to be served.

2.3 Vietnamese Herb Salad Recipe

Preparation Time: 10 minutes
Cooking Time: 30 minutes
Serving: 2

Ingredients:

- Parsley leaves, half pound
- Maple syrup, one teaspoon
- Sliced celery, a quarter teaspoon
- Fresh dill leaves, half cup
- Roasted cashews, half cup
- Pepper, as required
- Cilantro, half cup
- Salt, a quarter teaspoon
- Soy sauce, as required
- Basil leaves, half cup
- Fresh fruit as required
- Salad dressing, half cup

Instructions:

1. Peel the leaves and then cut them into large pieces.
2. Mix all the ingredients along with the leaves and fruits.
3. In a bowl, add the salad dressing and beat it well.
4. Drizzle the dressing on top of the leaves and fruit mixture.
5. Your dish is ready to be served.

2.4 Vietnamese Summer Rolls with Peanut Dipping Sauce Recipe

Preparation Time: 10 minutes
Cooking Time: 20 minutes
Serving: 2

Ingredients:

- Olive oil, two cups
- Garlic powder, one tablespoon
- Salt to taste
- Pepper to taste
- Paprika, one tablespoon
- Onion diced, one cup
- Parsley, one tablespoon
- Pork meat, one cup
- Tomatoes, one cup
- Jalapeno slices, as required
- Peanut dipping sauce, one cup
- Avocado slices, as required
- Tortilla sheets, four

Instructions:

1. Add the olive oil into a pan.
2. Heat the oil well.
3. Add the onions.
4. Cook the onions well until they turn soft.
5. Add parsley, garlic powder, paprika and tomatoes.
6. Cook them for five minutes.
7. Cook the mixture again and keep stirring.
8. Add pieces of pork meat.
9. Continue to cook the ingredients for few minutes.
10. Lay the mixture onto a tortilla sheet.
11. Add the peanut dipping sauce on top of the meat.
12. Add the rest of the ingredients on top and roll it into a roll.
13. Heat the roll.
14. You can serve it with any other sauce of your choice.
15. Your dish is ready to be served.

2.5 Vietnamese Pork Meatballs Recipe

Preparation Time: 30 minutes
Cooking Time: 10 minutes
Serving: 4

Ingredients:

- Soy sauce, two tablespoon
- Eggs, two
- Salt, to taste
- Black pepper, to taste
- Milk, one cup
- Onion, one cup

- Bread crumbs, one cup
- Sugar, two tablespoon
- Minced pork meat, one pound
- Minced ginger, two tablespoon
- Cayenne pepper, a dash
- Butter, two tablespoon
- All-purpose flour, five tablespoon

Instructions:
1. Take a large bowl.
2. Add the oil and onions into the bowl.
3. Add the chopped ginger into the bowl.
4. Add the minced pork into the bowl.
5. Add the spices, eggs and bread crumbs.
6. Mix all the ingredients together.
7. Shape the pork mixture into round meatballs.
8. Heat a grilling pan.
9. Add the olive oil on top.
10. Place the meatballs on top.
11. Fry the meatballs on both sides until it turns golden brown.
12. Fry all the meatballs and dish them out.
13. The dish is ready to be served.

2.6 Vietnamese Chicken Pho Recipe

Preparation Time: 30 minutes
Cooking Time: 20 minutes
Serving: 4

Ingredients:

- Shredded chicken, one cup
- Onion, one cup

- Rice noodles, one cup
- Chinese paprika, half teaspoon
- Water, one cup
- Minced garlic, two tablespoon
- Minced ginger, two tablespoon
- Cilantro, half cup
- Olive oil, two tablespoon
- Water, half cup
- Chicken stock, half cup
- Chopped tomatoes, one cup

Instructions:
1. Take a pan.
2. Add in the oil and onions.
3. Cook the onions until they become soft and fragrant.
4. Add in the chopped garlic and ginger.
5. Cook the mixture and add the tomatoes into it.
6. Add the spices.
7. When the tomatoes are done, add the shredded chicken and stock into it.
8. Mix the ingredients carefully and cover your pan.
9. Add the rice noodles into the mixture.
10. Add the water into the mixture and cover the pan.
11. Let the pho cook for ten to fifteen minutes straight.
12. Add cilantro on top.
13. Your dish is ready to be served.

2.7 Vietnamese Baked Snapper Recipe

Preparation Time: 10 minutes

Cooking Time: 25 minutes
Serving: 2

Ingredients:

- Powdered cumin, one tablespoon
- Salt, to taste
- Black pepper, to taste
- Turmeric powder, one teaspoon
- Onion, one cup
- Smoked paprika, half teaspoon
- Hoison sauce, half cup
- Snapper pieces, one pound
- Minced garlic, two tablespoon
- Minced ginger, two tablespoon
- Cilantro, half cup
- Olive oil, two tablespoon
- Oyster sauce, three tablespoon
- Roasted peanuts, half cup

Instructions:
1. Take a large bowl.
2. Add the oil and onions into the bowl.
3. Add the chopped garlic and ginger into the bowl.
4. Add the tomatoes into the bowl.
5. Add the spices.
6. Add the cilantro into it.
7. Mix all the ingredients together.
8. Cover your snapper pieces with the mixture above.
9. Bake your snapper pieces.
10. Dish them out when cooked properly.
11. Sprinkle some cilantro and roasted peanuts on top.

12.   You can serve it with any of your preferred sauces.

13.   Your dish is ready to be served.

2.8 Vietnamese Stir-Fried Sweet Shrimp Recipe

Preparation Time: 30 minutes
Cooking Time: 10 minutes
Serving: 4

Ingredients:

- Fish broth, one cup
- Honey, one teaspoon
- Onion, one cup
- Brown sugar, two tablespoon
- Smoked paprika, half teaspoon
- Water, one cup
- Shrimps, two cups
- Mixed spices, two tablespoon
- Minced garlic, two tablespoon
- Minced ginger, two tablespoon
- Cilantro, half cup
- Olive oil, two tablespoon
- Chopped tomatoes, one cup

Instructions:

1. Take a pan.
2. Add in the oil and onions.
3. Cook the onions until they become soft and fragrant.
4. Add in the chopped garlic and ginger.
5. Cook the mixture and add the tomatoes into it.

6. Add the spices, honey, sugar and sauces.

7. When the tomatoes are done, add the shrimps into it.

8. Cook for five minutes.

9. When cooked, dish it out.

10.   Garnish your dish with chopped cilantro leaves

11.   Your dish is ready to be served.

2.9 Vietnamese Lemongrass and Tamarind Chicken Recipe

Preparation Time: 30 minutes
Cooking Time: 10 minutes
Serving: 4

Ingredients:

- Cilantro, half cup
- Sesame oil, two tablespoon
- Chopped tomatoes, one cup
- Lemon juice, one cup
- Powdered cumin, one tablespoon
- Salt, to taste
- Black pepper, to taste
- Lemongrass, one teaspoon
- Onion, one cup
- Vegetable broth, one cup
- Chinese paprika, half teaspoon
- Chicken cubes, two cup
- Tamarind paste, half cup
- Minced garlic, two tablespoon
- Minced ginger, two tablespoon

Instructions:

1. Take a pan.
2. Add in the oil and onions.
3. Cook the onions until they become soft and fragrant.
4. Add in the chopped garlic and ginger.
5. Cook the mixture and add the tomatoes into it.
6. Add the spices.
7. When the tomatoes are done, add the chicken cubes into it.
8. Cook for five minutes.
9. Add in the lemongrass and tamarind paste.
10. Add in the broth and lemon juice.
11. Mix the ingredients carefully and cover the pan.
12. When cooked, dish it out.
13. Garnish the dish with chopped cilantro leaves
14. Your dish is ready to be served.

2.10 Vietnamese Marinated Lamb Chops Recipe

Preparation Time: 10 minutes
Cooking Time: 25 minutes
Serving: 2

Ingredients:

- Lemon juice, one tablespoon
- Salt, to taste

- Black pepper, to taste
- Mix spice, one teaspoon
- Onion, one cup
- Smoked paprika, half teaspoon
- Lamb chops, one pound
- Minced garlic, two tablespoon
- Minced ginger, two tablespoon
- Cilantro, half cup
- Olive oil, two tablespoon

Instructions:
1. Take a large bowl.
2. Add the oil and onions into the bowl.
3. Add the chopped garlic and ginger into the bowl.
4. Add the spices.
5. Add the cilantro into it.
6. Mix all the ingredients together.
7. Add the lamb chops into the mixture.
8. Cook the lamb chops.
9. Dish them out when cooked properly.
10. Sprinkle some cilantro on top.
11. Your dish is ready to be served.

2.11 Vietnamese Cabbage Soup Recipe

Preparation Time: 30 minutes
Cooking Time: 20 minutes
Serving: 4

Ingredients:

- Sliced cabbage, one cup
- Eggs, two
- Onion, one cup

- Chinese paprika, half teaspoon
- Water, one cup
- Minced garlic, two tablespoon
- Minced ginger, two tablespoon
- Cilantro, half cup
- Olive oil, two tablespoon
- Water, half cup
- Vegetable stock, half cup
- Chopped tomatoes, one cup

Instructions:

1. Take a pan.
2. Add in the oil and onions.
3. Cook the onions until they become soft and fragrant.
4. Add in the chopped garlic and ginger.
5. Cook the mixture and add the tomatoes into it.
6. Add the spices.
7. When the tomatoes are done, add the sliced cabbage and stock into it.
8. Mix the ingredients carefully and cover your pan.
9. Let the soup cook for ten to fifteen minutes straight.
10. Add cilantro on top.
11. Your dish is ready to be served.

2.12 Vietnamese Mixed Vegetables Recipe

Preparation Time: 30 minutes
Cooking Time: 10 minutes
Serving: 4

Ingredients:

- Chopped tomatoes, one cup
- Cauliflower, one cup
- Mix spice powder, one teaspoon
- Onion, one cup
- Fish sauce, a quarter cup
- Oyster sauce, a quarter cup
- Brussel sprouts, one cup
- Smoked paprika, half teaspoon
- Chopped carrots, one cup
- Minced garlic, two tablespoon
- Minced ginger, two tablespoon
- Lemon juice, half cup
- Chopped bell peppers, one cup
- Olive oil, two tablespoon

Instructions:

1. Take a pan.
2. Add in the oil and onions.
3. Cook the onions until they become soft and fragrant.
4. Add in the chopped garlic and ginger.
5. Cook the mixture and add the tomatoes to it.
6. Add the spices.
7. When the tomatoes are done, add the vegetables into it.
8. Mix the ingredients carefully and cover the pan.
9. When your vegetables are done, dish them out.
10. Add cilantro on top.
11. Your dish is ready to be served.

2.13 Vietnamese Fried Rice Recipe

Preparation Time: 10 minutes
Cooking Time: 25 minutes
Serving: 2

Ingredients:

- Minced garlic, two tablespoon
- Minced ginger, two tablespoon
- Cilantro, half cup
- Cooked rice, one cup
- Olive oil, two tablespoon
- Coconut cream, three tablespoon
- Chopped tomatoes, one cup
- Water, one cup
- Fish sauce, one teaspoon
- Onion, one cup
- Coconut milk, one cup
- Smoked paprika, half teaspoon
- Water, one cup

Instructions:
1. Take a pan.
2. Add in the oil and onions.
3. Cook the onions until they become soft and fragrant.
4. Add in the chopped garlic and ginger.
5. Cook the mixture and add the tomatoes into it.
6. Add the spices.
7. When the tomatoes are done, add the coconut milk into it.
8. Add in the water.
9. Mix the ingredients carefully and cover your pan.
10. Add in the rice and into the mixture.

11.   Fry the rice and let it cook for an additional five minutes.
12.   Add cilantro on top.
13.   Your dish is ready to be served.

2.14 Vietnamese Pork Chops Recipe

Preparation Time: 10 minutes
Cooking Time: 20 minutes
Serving: 2

Ingredients:

- Fish sauce, half teaspoon
- Water, half cup
- Pork chops, one pound
- Minced garlic, two tablespoon
- Minced ginger, two tablespoon
- Cilantro, half cup
- Olive oil, two tablespoon
- Chopped tomatoes, one cup
- Lemon juice, one cup
- Oyster sauce, one tablespoon
- Salt, to taste
- Black pepper, to taste
- Mix spice, one teaspoon
- Onion, one cup
- pork broth, one cup

Instructions:

1. Take a pan.
2. Add in the oil and onions.
3. Cook the onions until they become soft and fragrant.

4. Add in the chopped garlic and ginger.
5. Cook the mixture and add the tomatoes into it.
6. Add the spices.
7. When the tomatoes are done, add the pork chops into it.
8. Add in the water and lemon juice.
9. Mix the ingredients carefully and cover the pan.
10. Garnish the dish with chopped cilantro.
11. Your dish is ready to be served.

2.15 Vietnamese Instant Pho Soup Recipe

Preparation Time: 30 minutes
Cooking Time: 20 minutes
Serving: 4

Ingredients:

- Pork, two cup
- Onion, one cup
- Rice noodles, one cup
- Oyster sauce, half teaspoon
- Water, one cup
- Minced garlic, two tablespoon
- Minced ginger, two tablespoon
- Cilantro, half cup
- Fish sauce, two tablespoon
- Olive oil, two tablespoon
- Chicken stock, half cup
- Chopped tomatoes, one cup

Instructions:
1. Take an instant pot.
2. Add in the oil and onions.

3. Cook the onions until they become soft and fragrant.
4. Add in the chopped garlic and ginger.
5. Cook the mixture and add the tomatoes into it.
6. Add the spices.
7. When the tomatoes are done, add the minced pork and stock into it.
8. Mix the ingredients carefully and cover your pot.
9. Let the pho cook for ten to fifteen minutes straight.
10. Add the rice noodles into the pot and cook for five minutes.
11. Add cilantro on top.
12. Your dish is ready to be served.

Chapter 3: The World of Vietnamese Dinner Recipes

Vegetables and noodles are the standard eating routine in many families in the cities of Vietnam. A typical Vietnamese feast will usually incorporate rice, a meat or fish dish, soups and vegetables. Following are some classic dinner recipes that are rich in healthy nutrients and you can easily make them with the detailed instructions list in each recipe:

3.1 Vietnamese Sambal Kangkung with Shrimp Paste Recipe

Preparation Time: 30 minutes
Cooking Time: 10 minutes
Serving: 4

Ingredients:

- Sambal olek, one tablespoon
- Cilantro, half cup
- Sesame oil, two tablespoon
- Chopped tomatoes, one cup
- shrimp paste, one cup
- Powdered cumin, one tablespoon
- Salt, to taste
- Black pepper, to taste
- Lemongrass, one teaspoon
- Chinese paprika, half teaspoon
- Diced kangkung, one pound
- Tamarind paste, half cup
- Minced garlic, two tablespoon
- Minced ginger, two tablespoon

Instructions:

1. Take a pan.
2. Add in the oil and onions.
3. Cook the onions until they become soft and fragrant.
4. Add in the chopped garlic and ginger.
5. Cook the mixture and add the tomatoes into it.
6. Add the spices.
7. When the tomatoes are done, add the kangkung and shrimp paste into it.
8. Cook for five minutes.
9. Add in the sambal olek, lemongrass and tamarind paste.
10. Mix the ingredients carefully and cover the pan.
11. When cooked, dish it out.
12. Garnish the dish with chopped cilantro leaves
13. Your dish is ready to be served.

3.2 Vietnamese Pomelo and Shrimp Salad Recipe

Preparation Time: 10 minutes
Cooking Time: 30 minutes
Serving: 2

Ingredients:

- Cooked shrimps, half pound
- Bean sprouts, one cup
- Sliced celery, a quarter teaspoon
- Fresh basil leaves, half cup

- Pomelo pulp, half cup
- Pepper, as required
- Cilantro, half cup
- Salt, a quarter teaspoon
- Soy sauce, as required
- Bird's eye chili, half cup
- Salad dressing, half cup

Instructions:
1. Cut the bean sprouts into large pieces.
2. Mix all the ingredients along with the shrimps.
3. In a bowl, add the salad dressing and beat it well.
4. Drizzle the dressing on top of the shrimps.
5. Your dish is ready to be served.

3.3 Vietnamese Pork Bone and Green Papaya Soup Recipe

Preparation Time: 10 minutes
Cooking Time: 10 minutes
Serving: 4

Ingredients:

- Chopped white onions, one cup
- Chopped green papaya, one pound
- Chicken stock, one quart
- Unsalted butter, three tablespoon
- Pork bones, half pound
- Fresh cilantro, as required
- Fresh herbs, half cup
- Dried thyme, one teaspoon
- Minced garlic, one teaspoon
- Fish sauce, half teaspoon

- Oyster sauce, two tablespoon

Instructions:
1. Take a large pan.
2. Add the chopped onions in the butter.
3. When soft and translucent, add in the minced garlic.
4. Add in the stock, and rest of the ingredients.
5. Add in all the rest of the ingredients and cook the ingredients until the papaya is cooked.
6. Remove the bone pieces.
7. Blend the soup well.
8. Cook the soup for an extra few minutes.
9. Add the soup in a serving bowl.
10. You can also garnish it with chopped fresh cilantro.
11. The dish is ready to be served.

3.4 Vietnamese Beef and Noodle Salad Recipe

Preparation Time: 10 minutes
Cooking Time: 25 minutes
Serving: 4

Ingredients:

- Cooked beef cubes, one cup
- Carrot sliced, one cup
- Red bell pepper sliced, one cup
- Ginger, one tablespoon
- Garlic powder, two teaspoon
- Fish sauce, half teaspoon
- Sesame oil, one teaspoon
- Soy sauce, one teaspoon

- Sriracha, one tablespoon
- Lime juice, one tablespoon
- Rice noodles, one pack
- Salt, to taste
- Pepper, to taste

Instructions:
1. Take a large bowl and add beef cubes into it.
2. Add the ginger and garlic powder.
3. Mix well.
4. Add the carrot slices and red bell pepper into it.
5. Add the salt and pepper as you like.
6. Add the sesame oil and mix well so that a homogeneous mixture is obtained.
7. Add the sriracha and rest of the ingredients into the mixture.
8. Mix all the ingredients.
9. Your salad is ready to be served.

3.5 Vietnamese Lamb Shanks with Sweet Potatoes Recipe

Preparation Time: 30 minutes
Cooking Time: 10 minutes
Serving: 4

Ingredients:

- Cooked sweet potatoes, two cup
- Mix spice, one teaspoon
- Onion, one cup
- Smoked paprika, half teaspoon
- Chinese dried chilies, half cup
- Minced garlic, two tablespoon
- Minced ginger, two tablespoon

- Lemon juice, half cup
- Oyster sauce, half cup
- Lamb shanks, half pound
- Olive oil, two tablespoon
- Chopped tomatoes, one cup

Instructions:
1. Take a pan.
2. Add in the oil and onions.
3. Cook the onions until they become soft and fragrant.
4. Add in the chopped garlic and ginger.
5. Cook the mixture and add the tomatoes into it.
6. Add the spices.
7. When the tomatoes are done, add the sweet potato and rest of the ingredients into it.
8. Mix the ingredients carefully.
9. Add cilantro on top.
10. Your dish is ready to be served.

3.6 Vietnamese Spiced Duck Salad Recipe

Preparation Time: 10 minutes
Cooking Time: 10 minutes
Serving: 2

Ingredients:

- Roasted duck, half pound
- Spicy red sauce, one cup
- Sliced celery, a quarter teaspoon
- Fresh basil leaves, half cup
- Sirarcha, half cup
- Pepper, as required
- Cilantro, half cup
- Salt, a quarter teaspoon
- Soy sauce, as required
- Bird's eye chili, half cup
- Salad dressing, half cup

Instructions:

1. Cut the duck meat into large pieces.
2. Mix all the ingredients along with the duck meat.
3. In a bowl, add the salad dressing and beat it well.
4. Drizzle the dressing on top of the meat.
5. Your dish is ready to be served.

3.7 Vietnamese Seafood Salad Recipe

Preparation Time: 10 minutes
Cooking Time: 10 minutes
Serving: 2

Ingredients:

- Mixed seafood, half pound
- Wine vinegar, one cup
- Caster sugar, a quarter teaspoon
- Spring onions, half cup
- Bean sprouts, two cups
- Sirarcha, half cup
- Pepper, as required
- Cilantro, half cup
- Salt, a quarter teaspoon
- Soy sauce, as required
- Bird's eye chili, half cup
- Salad dressing, half cup

Instructions:
1. Cook your seafood by boiling it well.
2. Mix all the ingredients along with the bean sprouts and spring onions.
3. In a bowl, add the salad dressing and beat it well.
4. Drizzle the dressing on top of the mixture.
5. Your dish is ready to be served.

3.8 Vietnamese Caramel Trout Recipe

Preparation Time: 30 minutes
Cooking Time: 10 minutes
Serving: 4

Ingredients:

- Brown sugar, one tablespoon
- Cilantro, half cup
- Sesame oil, two tablespoon
- Chopped tomatoes, one cup
- Rainbow trout, one cup
- Oyster sauce, one tablespoon
- Salt, to taste
- Black pepper, to taste
- Lemongrass, one teaspoon
- Chinese paprika, half teaspoon
- Steamed rice, one cup
- Minced garlic, two tablespoon
- Minced ginger, two tablespoon

Instructions:
1. Take a pan.
2. Add in the oil and onions.
3. Cook the onions until they become soft and fragrant.
4. Add in the chopped garlic and ginger.
5. Cook the mixture and add the tomatoes into it.
6. Add the spices.
7. When the tomatoes are done, add the trout into it.
8. Cook for five minutes.
9. Add in the brown sugar, lemongrass and steamed rice.
10. Mix the ingredients carefully and cover the pan.
11. When cooked, dish it out.

12.   Garnish the dish with chopped cilantro leaves.

13.   Your dish is ready to be served.

3.9 Vietnamese Veggie Hotpot Recipe

Preparation Time: 20 minutes
Cooking Time: 20 minutes
Serving: 4

Ingredients:

- Oyster sauce, one tablespoon
- Chinese chili peppers, two
- Fish sauce, one tablespoon
- Soy sauce, half tablespoon
- Minced garlic, two teaspoon
- Cooking oil, three tablespoon
- Hot sauce, half cup
- Mixed vegetables, two cups
- Salt, as required
- Chopped fresh cilantro, as required

Instructions:
1. Take a large pan.
2. Add the cooking oil into the pan and heat it.
3. Add the vegetables into the pan and stir-fry it.
4. Add the minced garlic along with the vegetables.
5. Add the soy sauce, fish sauce, Chinese chili peppers, hot sauce and rest of the ingredients into the mixture.
6. Cook your dish for ten minutes.
7. Dish out your vegetables and garnish them with chopped fresh cilantro leaves.

8. Your dish is ready to be served.

3.10 Vietnamese Prawn and Noodle Salad with Crispy Shallots Recipe

Preparation Time: 10 minutes
Cooking Time: 25 minutes
Serving: 4

Ingredients:

- Cooked prawns, one cup
- Carrot sliced, one cup
- Red bell pepper sliced, one cup
- Ginger, one tablespoon
- Garlic powder, two teaspoon
- Fish sauce, half teaspoon
- Sesame oil, one teaspoon
- Soy sauce, one teaspoon
- Sriracha, one tablespoon
- Lime juice, one tablespoon
- Rice noodles, one pack
- Salt, to taste
- Pepper, to taste
- Shallots, half cup

Instructions:
1. Take a large bowl and add prawns into it.
2. Add the ginger and garlic powder.
3. Mix well.
4. Add the carrot slices and red bell pepper into it.
5. Add the salt and pepper as you like.
6. Add the sesame oil and mix well so that a homogeneous mixture is obtained.

7. Add the sriracha and rest of the ingredients into the mixture.
8. Fry the shallots in oil until they turn crispy.
9. Add the shallots on top of the mixture.
10.   Your salad is ready to be served.

3.11 Vietnamese Lemongrass Chicken Recipe

Preparation Time: 30 minutes
Cooking Time: 10 minutes
Serving: 4

Ingredients:

- Cilantro, half cup
- Sesame oil, two tablespoon
- Chopped tomatoes, one cup
- Lemon juice, one cup
- Fish sauce, one tablespoon
- Salt, to taste
- Black pepper, to taste
- Lemongrass, one teaspoon
- Onion, one cup
- Vegetable broth, one cup
- Chinese paprika, half teaspoon
- Chicken cubes, two cup
- Minced garlic, two tablespoon
- Minced ginger, two tablespoon

Instructions:
1. Take a pan.
2. Add in the oil and onions.
3. Cook the onions until they become soft and fragrant.

4. Add in the chopped garlic and ginger.

5. Cook the mixture and add the tomatoes into it.

6. Add the spices.

7. When the tomatoes are done, add the chicken cubes into it.

8. Cook for five minutes.

9. Add in the lemongrass.

10. Add in the broth and lemon juice.

11. Mix the ingredients carefully and cover the pan.

12. When cooked, dish it out.

13. Garnish the dish with chopped cilantro leaves

14. Your dish is ready to be served.

3.12 Vietnamese Garlic Butter Noodles Recipe

Preparation Time: 30 minutes
Cooking Time: 10 minutes
Serving: 4

Ingredients:

- Butter, one tablespoon
- Cilantro, one cup
- Fresh ginger, one teaspoon
- Fish sauce, one tablespoon
- Soy sauce, one tablespoon
- Oyster sauce, half teaspoon
- Chili garlic sauce, two tablespoon
- Fresh cilantro leaves, half cup
- Fresh basil leaves, a quarter cup
- Vegetable broth, one cup

- Rice noodles, as required

Instructions:
1. Add all the ingredients of the sauce into a wok.
2. Cook your ingredients.
3. Add the noodles into the mixture once the sauce is ready.
4. Mix the noodles well and cook it for five minutes.
5. Add the cilantro into the dish.
6. Your dish is ready to be served.

3.13 Vietnamese Papaya Salad Recipe

Preparation Time: 10 minutes
Cooking Time: 30 minutes
Serving: 2

Ingredients:

- Maple syrup, one teaspoon
- Ground ginger, a quarter teaspoon
- Papaya, two
- Mixed nuts, two tablespoon
- Pepper, as required
- Cilantro, half cup
- Salt, a quarter teaspoon
- Soy sauce, as required
- Mint leaves, half cup
- Salad dressing, half cup

Instructions:

7. Peel the papaya and then cut into large pieces.
8. Mix all the ingredients along with the papaya.
9. In a bowl, add the salad dressing and beat it well.
10.   Drizzle the dressing on top of the papaya mixture.
11.   Your dish is ready to be served.

3.14 Vietnamese Purple Yam Soup Recipe

Preparation Time: 10 minutes
Cooking Time: 30 minutes
Serving: 4

Ingredients:

- Chopped white onions, one cup
- Purple yam, one pound
- Fresh chopped cilantro, half cup
- Unsalted butter, three tablespoon
- Oyster sauce, one teaspoon
- Minced garlic, one teaspoon
- Fish sauce, half teaspoon
- Coconut milk, half cup
- Coconut cream, one cup

Instructions:
1. In a large pan, add the chopped onions in the butter.
2. Add in the minced garlic when onions are soft and translucent.
3. Add in the purple yam.
4. Add in all the rest of the ingredients and cook the ingredients until the purple yams are cooked.
5. Blend the soup well.

6. Cook for an extra few minutes.
7. The dish is ready to be served.

3.15 Vietnamese Fried Tofu Recipe

Preparation Time: 30 minutes
Cooking Time: 10 minutes
Serving: 4

Ingredients:

- Cilantro, half cup
- Olive oil, two tablespoon
- Chopped tomatoes, one cup
- Lemon juice, half cup
- Mix spice powder, one tablespoon
- Salt, to taste
- Black pepper, to taste
- Fish sauce, one teaspoon
- Onion, one cup
- Tofu cubes, one cup
- Oyster sauce, half teaspoon
- Minced garlic, two tablespoon

Instructions:

1. Take a pan.
2. Add in the oil and onions.
3. Cook the onions until they become soft and fragrant.
4. Add in the chopped garlic.
5. Cook the mixture and add the tomatoes into it.
6. Add the spices and sauces.
7. When the tomatoes are done, add the tofu cubes into it.
8. Cook for five minutes.

9. When cooked, dish it out.
10.   Garnish your dish with chopped cilantro leaves.
11.   Your dish is ready to be served.

3.16 Vietnamese Noodle Soup Recipe

Preparation Time: 10 minutes
Cooking Time: 20 minutes
Serving: 4

Ingredients:

- Minced garlic, two tablespoon
- Minced ginger, two tablespoon
- Cilantro, half cup
- Diced carrots, one cup
- Olive oil, two tablespoon
- Beef broth, half cup
- Fish sauce, half cup
- Vegetable stock, half cup
- Chopped tomatoes, one cup
- Chicken broth, one cup
- Hot sauce, half cup
- Onion, one cup
- Bell peppers, one cup
- Noodles, half pound
- Oyster sauce, half teaspoon
- Soy sauce, one cup

Instructions:

1. Take a pan.
2. Add in the oil and onions.

3. Cook the onions until they become soft and fragrant.
4. Add in the chopped garlic and ginger.
5. Cook the mixture and add the tomatoes into it.
6. Add the sauces.
7. When the tomatoes are done, add the noodles into it.
8. Add in both chicken and beef broth.
9. Mix the ingredients carefully and cover your pan.
10. Add the vegetables into the mixture.
11. Add the water into the mixture and cover the pan.
12. Let the soup cook for ten to fifteen minutes straight.
13. Add the cilantro on top.
14. Your dish is ready to be served.

3.17 Vietnamese Shaking Beef Recipe

Preparation Time: 30 minutes
Cooking Time: 20 minutes
Serving: 4

Ingredients:

- Sesame oil, two tablespoon
- Sugar, one teaspoon
- Oyster sauce, two tablespoon
- Pepper to taste
- Salt, as required
- Chinese cooking wine, two teaspoon
- Soy sauce, two tablespoon
- Beef, two pounds
- Vegetable oil, two tablespoon

- Cornstarch, two tablespoon

Instructions:
1. Add the oil in a large pan.
2. Add in the beef and cook it properly.
3. Add the rest of the ingredients.
4. In the end add the cornstarch and once the dish thickens, switch off the heat.
5. Your dish is ready to be served.

3.18 Vietnamese Tomato and Pineapple Fish Soup Recipe

Preparation Time: 30 minutes
Cooking Time: 20 minutes
Serving: 4

Ingredients:

- Diced pineapple, one cup
- Deboned fish, two cups
- Onion, one cup
- Oyster sauce, half teaspoon
- Water, one cup
- Minced garlic, two tablespoon
- Soy sauce, two tablespoon
- Cilantro, half cup
- Olive oil, two tablespoon
- Water, half cup
- Vegetable stock, half cup
- Cherry tomatoes, one cup

Instructions:
1. Take a pan.
2. Add in the oil and onions.
3. Cook the onions until they become soft and fragrant.
4. Add in the chopped garlic.
5. Cook the mixture and add the cherry tomatoes into it.
6. Add the spices and sauces.
7. When the tomatoes are done, add the diced pineapple and fish into it.
8. Mix in the rest of the ingredients and cover your pan.
9. Let the soup cook for ten to fifteen minutes straight.
10. Add cilantro on top.
11. Your dish is ready to be served.

Chapter 4: The World of Vietnamese Dessert Recipes

If you are a dessert lover and want to enjoy new flavors and tastes, you are in for a treat with various Vietnamese sweets. Ordinarily low in sugar and made with solid ingredients, you will track down a wide collection of sweet alternatives in the Vietnamese cuisine. Following are some yummy dessert recipes that are rich in healthy nutrients:

4.1 Vietnamese Pandan Rice and Mung Bean Cake Recipe

Preparation Time: 10 minutes
Cooking Time: 20 minutes
Serving: 4

Ingredients:

- Sweet pandan rice, two cup
- Salt, a pinch
- Bread flour, half cup
- Coconut milk, one cup
- Lime zest, as required
- Pepper, to taste
- Mung bean paste, one cup
- Baking powder, one teaspoon
- Vanilla essence, half teaspoon
- Soy sauce, one tablespoon

Instructions:
1. Add the bread flour into a large bowl.

2. Cook the pandan rice in the rice cooking pan.
3. Add the rice into the bowl when it is cooked. Then mix them.
4. Add the lime zest as required.
5. Add the cilantro if required.
6. Add some water and boil the whole mixture for ten minutes.
7. Cool the mixture and then add the vanilla essence, baking powder and coconut milk into it.
8. Mix the ingredients.
9. Add the batter into the cupcake molds.
10. Add the mung bean paste in the center of the mixture.
11. Bake the rice cake.
12. Dish out the cake when it is done.
13. Your dish is ready to be served.

4.2 Vietnamese Peanut Sticky Rice Recipe

Preparation Time: 20 minutes
Cooking Time: 20 minutes
Serving: 4

Ingredients:

- Cooked rice, one bowl
- Cilantro, as required
- Baking powder, four teaspoon
- Coconut flakes, one and a half cup
- Baking soda, one teaspoon
- Buttermilk, two cups
- Peanut essence, two drops
- Roasted peanuts, one cup

- White sugar, one cup
- Water, two cups
- Tapioca flour, one cup
- Coconut cream, half cup

Instructions:
1. Add the tapioca flour into a large bowl.
2. Add the white sugar into the mixture as required.
3. Add the baking powder and beat the mixture for five more minutes.
4. Add the water in a separate bowl.
5. Add coconut flakes into it.
6. Add the coconut cream into the mixture.
7. Add the cooked rice into it.
8. Mix them thoroughly until a homogeneous mixture is obtained.
9. Add the peanut essence and roasted peanuts.
10. Mix the rice well.
11. Your dish is ready to be served.

4.3 Vietnamese Mung Bean Dumplings Recipe

Preparation Time: 50 minutes
Cooking Time: 30 minutes
Serving: 4

Ingredients:

- Mung bean paste, two cups
- Thin soy sauce, one tablespoon
- Cinnamon powder, half tablespoon
- Sweet vinegar, one tablespoon

- Milk, one cup
- Vegetable oil, one tablespoon
- All-purpose flour, one cup
- Whole wheat flour, half cup
- Salt, to taste
- Water, to knead

Instructions:

1. Take a bowl and add the flour into it.
2. Add lukewarm water in it.
3. Set aside for half an hour.
4. Take the whole wheat flour.
5. Then add the salt and milk in it.
6. Then combine the ingredients to form a soft dough.
7. Kneed it for ten minutes.
8. Take a small bowl.
9. Add the thin soy sauce, cinnamon powder, sweet vinegar and mung bean paste in the bowl.
10. Make round forms of dough with the help of the oil.
11. Add the mung bean mixture in between.
12. Steam your dumplings for ten minutes.
13. Once the dumplings are steamed, take them out.
14. Your dish is ready to be served.

4.4 Vietnamese Pandan Waffles Recipe

Preparation Time: 30 minutes
Cooking Time: 10 minutes
Serving: 4

Ingredients:

- Rice flour, one cup
- Eggs, two
- Chopped fresh cilantro, half cup
- Coconut milk, one cup
- Salt to taste
- Pandan leaves, half cup
- Pandan essence, two tablespoon

Instructions:

1. Heat your waffle maker.
2. Beat the egg yolks in a separate bowl.
3. Add in the egg yolks in the egg whites and delicately mix them with a spatula.
4. Combine the eggs and the rest of the ingredients.
5. When your waffle maker is heated adequately, pour in the mixture.
6. Close your waffle maker.
7. Let your waffle cook for five to six minutes approximately.
8. When your waffles are done, dish them out.
9. Add the chopped cilantro leaves on top of the waffles.
10. Your dish is ready to be served.

4.5 Vietnamese Three Color Dessert Recipe

Preparation Time: 10 minutes
Cooking Time: 20 minutes

Serving: 4

Ingredients:

- Green color, three drops
- Red color, three drops
- Yellow color, three drops
- Rice, one cup
- Baking powder, four teaspoon
- Coconut milk, one cup
- All-purpose flour, one and a half cup
- Baking soda, one teaspoon
- Eggs, two
- Brown sugar, one cup
- Tapioca starch, one tablespoon
- Salt, to taste

Instructions:
1. Add the eggs in a large bowl.
2. Beat the eggs until they turn frothy.
3. Add the baking powder and coconut milk into it.
4. Add the brown sugar and beat the mixture for five more minutes.
5. In a separate bowl, add all the dried ingredients.
6. Mix them thoroughly.
7. Cook your mixture until it turns thick.
8. Cook the rice in rice cooking pan.
9. Divide the rice in three portions and add the colors.
10. Add the rice into the formed mixture.
11. Your dish is ready to be served.
12.

4.6 Vietnamese Fruit Cocktail Recipe

Preparation Time: 10 minutes
Cooking Time: 20 minutes
Serving: 4

Ingredients:

- Strawberries, half cup
- Banana slices, one cup
- Plain yogurt, half cup
- Milk, half cup
- Apples, half cup
- Melon, half cup
- Mixed fruit juice, half cup
- Ice cubes, as required

Instructions:
1. Take a blender and add the milk into it.
2. Add the banana slices into it.
3. Blend it for few minutes.
4. Then add the plain yogurt into it.
5. Add the fruit juice into it.
6. In the end, add the strawberries, melon and apples into it.
7. Your dish is ready to be served.

4.7 Vietnamese Sweet Corn Pudding Recipe

Preparation Time: 10 minutes
Cooking Time: 20 minutes
Serving: 4

Ingredients:

- Sweet corn, one cup
- Baking powder, four teaspoon
- Barley flakes, one and a half cup
- Baking soda, one teaspoon
- Buttermilk, two cups
- White sugar, one cup
- Water, two cups
- Tapioca flour, one cup
- Coconut cream, half cup

Instructions:

1. Add the tapioca flour into a large bowl.
2. Add the sweet corns into the mixture.
3. Add the white sugar and beat the mixture for five more minutes.
4. In a separate bowl, add all the dried ingredients.
5. Add the water into it
6. Add the coconut cream into the mixture.
7. Mix them thoroughly until a consistent mixture is formed.
8. Check the thickness of pudding and add extra sugar if required.
9. Your dish is ready to be served.

4.8 Vietnamese Banana Tapioca Recipe

Preparation Time: 10 minutes
Cooking Time: 20 minutes
Serving: 4

Ingredients:

- Sliced bananas, one cup
- Rice, one cup
- Baking powder, four teaspoon
- Coconut milk, one cup
- All-purpose flour, one and a half cup
- Baking soda, one teaspoon
- Eggs, two
- Brown sugar, one cup
- Tapioca starch, one tablespoon
- Salt, to taste

Instructions:
1. Add the eggs in a large bowl.
2. Beat the eggs until they turn frothy.
3. Add the baking powder and coconut milk into it.
4. Add the brown sugar and beat the mixture for five more minutes.
5. Add all the dried ingredients in a separate bowl.
6. Mix both the dried and wet ingredients thoroughly.
7. Cook the mixture.
8. Add the rice into the mixture and cook.
9. Put the banana slices on cooked rice.
10. Your dish is ready to be served.

4.9 Vietnamese Sesame Balls Recipe

Preparation Time: 10 minutes
Cooking Time: 40 minutes
Serving: 4

Ingredients:

- Salted butter, one cup
- Black sesame seeds, one cup
- Yeast, one tablespoon
- Large eggs, two
- Kosher salt, half teaspoon
- Almond slices, one cup
- Vanilla extract, one teaspoon
- Flour, three and a half cup
- White sugar, half cup

Instructions:
1. Take a large bowl and put the black sesame seeds into it.
2. Add the dry ingredients in the bowl.
3. Mix all the ingredients well.
4. Add the white sugar and yeast in a bowl with two tablespoon of hot water.
5. Place the yeast mixture in a damp place.
6. Add the butter into the wet ingredients.
7. Add the yeast mixture, sliced almonds and eggs into the cookie mixture.
8. Add the formed mixture into a pipping bag.
9. Make small round balls on a baking dish and bake the balls.
10. Your dish is ready to be served.

4.10 Vietnamese Sponge Cake Recipe

Preparation Time: 30 minutes
Cooking Time: 25 minutes
Serving: 4

Ingredients:

- Vanilla sauce, one cup
- Butter, half cup
- Sugar, a quarter cup
- Ground cardamom, a quarter teaspoon
- Flour, one cup
- Baking soda, a pinch
- Egg, one

Instructions:

1. Make the cake batter by mixing all the ingredients in a large bowl.
2. Make the batter and pour it into a baking dish.
3. Make sure the baking dish is properly greased and lined with parchment papers.
4. Bake the cake.
5. When cooked, dish it out.
6. Cut the cake into slices.
7. The dish is ready to be served.

4.11 Vietnamese Milkshake Recipe

Preparation Time: 10 minutes
Cooking Time: 20 minutes
Serving: 4

Ingredients:

- Avocado cubes, half cup
- Banana slices, one cup
- Plain yogurt, half cup
- Milk, half cup
- Coconut milk, half cup
- Ice cubes, as required

Instructions:
1. Take a blender and add the milk into it.
2. Add the banana slices into it.
3. Blend it for few minutes.
4. Then add the plain yogurt into it.
5. Add the coconut milk into it.
6. In the end, add the avocado cubes into it.
7. Blend the milkshake well.
8. Your dish is ready to be served.

4.12 Vietnamese Ice Cream Recipe

Preparation Time: 10 minutes
Cooking Time: 20 minutes
Serving: 4

Ingredients:

- Coffee paste, half cup
- Whole milk, half cup
- Cocoa powder, two tablespoon
- Rock sugar, half cup
- Vanilla extract, one teaspoon

Instructions:

1. Take a bowl and add the milk into it.
2. Add the sugar as required.
3. Mix them thoroughly.
4. Heat the mixture, and add the coffee paste into it.
5. Refrigerate your mixture for one night.
6. Put the cocoa powder on it.
7. Your dish is ready to be served.

4.13 Vietnamese Taro Pudding Recipe

Preparation Time: 10 minutes
Cooking Time: 20 minutes
Serving: 4

Ingredients:

- Taro roots, one cup
- Baking powder, four teaspoon
- Barley flakes, one and a half cup
- Baking soda, one teaspoon
- Buttermilk, two cups
- White sugar, one cup
- Water, two cups
- Tapioca flour, one cup
- Coconut cream, half cup

Instructions:

1. Add the tapioca flour into a large bowl.
2. Add the taro roots into the mixture.

3. Add the white sugar and beat the mixture for five more minutes.
4. In a separate bowl, add all the dried ingredients.
5. Add the water into it
6. Add the coconut cream into the mixture.
7. Mix them thoroughly until a homogeneous mixture is obtained.
8. Check the thickness of pudding and add extra sugar if required.
9. Your dish is ready to be served.

4.14 Vietnamese Sticky Rice Recipe

Preparation Time: 20 minutes
Cooking Time: 20 minutes
Serving: 4

Ingredients:

- Cooked rice, one bowl
- Cilantro, as required
- Baking soda, four teaspoon
- Coconut flakes, one and a half cup
- Baking soda, one teaspoon
- Buttermilk, two cups
- White sugar, one cup

- Water, two cups
- Tapioca flour, one cup
- Coconut cream, half cup

Instructions:
1. Add the tapioca flour into a large bowl.
2. Add the white sugar into the mixture as required.
3. Add the baking soda and beat the mixture for five more minutes.
4. In a separate bowl, add the water in it.
5. Add coconut flakes into it.
6. Add the coconut cream into the mixture.
7. Add the cooked rice into it.
8. Mix them thoroughly until a homogeneous mixture is obtained.
9. Mix the rice well.
10. Your dish is ready to be served.

4.15 Vietnamese Donuts Recipe

Preparation Time: 50 minutes
Cooking Time: 40 minutes
Serving: 2

Ingredients:

- Eggs, two
- Yeast, half cup
- Sesame powder, one tablespoon
- Maple syrup, one tablespoon
- Coconut milk, half cup
- White sugar, half cup

- Salt, one teaspoon
- Vanilla extract, one tablespoon
- Cake flour, two cups
- Butter, one cup

Instructions:
1. Take a medium bowl and add the eggs, sesame powder and the cake flour in it.
2. Add the one cup coconut milk and mix well.
3. Add the sugar, the salt and the beaten eggs.
4. Mix them well.
5. Mix the warm milk mixture with the flour and the coconut.
6. Add the eggs and vanilla extract together.
7. Add the yeast into the whole mixture.
8. When dough is formed, roll it in your desired shape.
9. Place the donuts on a greased baking tray.
10. Bake the donuts for twenty minutes.
11. Your dish is ready to be served.

Chapter 5: The World of Vietnamese Snack Recipes

Vietnamese snacks have a deep rooted place in the culture of Vietnam. Following are some amazing Vietnamese snack recipes that are rich in healthy nutrients and you can easily make them with the detailed instructions list in each recipe:

5.1 Crispy Vietnamese Fish Cakes Recipe

Preparation Time: 30 minutes
Cooking Time: 25 minutes
Serving: 4

Ingredients:

- All-purpose flour, one cup
- Crab meat, one cup
- Baking powder, one tablespoon
- Baking soda, half tablespoon
- Egg, two
- Milk, one cup
- Bread crumbs, one cup
- Vegetable oil, one cup
- Salt, half tablespoon
- Oil, one cup

Instructions:
1. Take a large bowl and add the all-purpose flour in it
2. Add the crab meat in it and mix well.
3. Add the baking powder, and salt into it.
4. Mix well until a good mixture is obtained.

5. Take another bowl and add the eggs into it.
6. Add the milk and a little oil into it.
7. Combine them well so that good mixture is formed.
8. Form round balls from the crab mixture and then dip them into the egg mixture.
9. Coat them with the bread crumbs.
10. Fry the balls until a light brown color comes.
11. Serve the cakes with your preferred sauce or dip.
12. Your dish is ready to be served.

5.2 Crispy Vietnamese Lettuce Cups Recipe

Preparation Time: 20 minutes
Cooking Time: 10 minutes
Serving: 4

Ingredients:

- Chopped coriander, a quarter cup
- Mint leaves, half cup
- Lettuce leaves, as required
- Cooked beef, one cup
- Lemongrass, one tablespoon
- Garlic powder, one tablespoon
- Milk, one cup
- Vegetable oil, one tablespoon
- Lemon juice, half cup
- Fish sauce, half cup
- Fried shallots, one tablespoon
- Salt, to taste
- Black pepper, as required
- Brown sugar, one tablespoon

- Cucumber, one cup
- Cooked noodles, one cup

Instructions:
1. Take a large bowl.
2. Add all the ingredients together into the bowl except the lettuce wraps.
3. Mix all the ingredients well to form a mixture.
4. Add the mixture into the lettuce wraps.
5. Fold the lettuce wraps.
6. Serve your wraps with soy sauce or any other sauce or dip you prefer.
7. Your dish is ready to be served.

5.3 Vietnamese Beef and Mango Salad Recipe

Preparation Time: 10 minutes
Cooking Time: 20 minutes
Serving: 4

Ingredients:

- Vietnamese salad dressing, two cups
- Minced ginger, two tablespoon
- Lemon juice, half cup
- Cilantro, one cup
- Olive oil, two tablespoon
- Chopped tomatoes, one cup
- Beef chunks, one cup
- Turmeric powder, one teaspoon
- Onion, one cup
- Mango cubes, one cup
- Soy sauce, half teaspoon

- Chopped avocado, one cup
- Minced garlic, two tablespoon

Instructions:
1. Peel and cut the mango into cubes.
2. Take a pan.
3. Add in the oil and onions.
4. Cook the onions until they become soft and fragrant.
5. Add in the chopped garlic and ginger.
6. Cook the mixture and add the tomatoes into it.
7. Add the spices.
8. When the tomatoes are done, add the beef chunks into it.
9. Mix the ingredients carefully.
10. When your beef is done, dish them out.
11. Peel and cut the avocado.
12. Place the chopped avocado and beef in a bowl.
13. Mix all the ingredients together.
14. Add the Vietnamese salad dressing on top of the salad.
15. Garnish your salad with the chopped cilantro.
16. Your dish is ready to be served.

5.4 Vietnamese Prawn and Lime Mayo Wrap Recipe

Preparation Time: 30 minutes
Cooking Time: 10 minutes
Serving: 4

Ingredients:

- Olive oil, half cup
- Chopped parsley, half cup
- Fish sauce, half cup
- Grated ginger, two tablespoon
- Lemon juice, two tablespoon
- Cabbage leaves, as required
- Cooked and shredded prawn meat, one cup
- Chopped orange, one
- Shredded carrots, one cup
- Green onion, one cup
- Chopped bell peppers, a quarter cup
- Orange juice, half cup
- Tortilla wraps, as required
- Lime mayo sauce, as required
- Balsamic vinegar, half cup

Instructions:

1. Add the balsamic vinegar, orange juice, chopped parsley, rosemary stalks, grated ginger, fish sauce and lemon juice in a large bowl.
2. Mix the ingredients together and keep it aside.
3. In the next bowl, add in the rest of the ingredients and mix well.
4. Add the sauce formed above.
5. Mix your filling and sauce.
6. Add the salad mixture onto your tortilla wraps and roll it.

7. Heat the wrap and drizzle extra sauce on top of the wrap.
8. Your dish is ready to be served.

5.5 Vietnamese Rice Paper Rolls Recipe

Preparation Time: 30 minutes
Cooking Time: 50 minutes
Serving: 4

Ingredients:

- Ginger, one tablespoon
- Rice paper, as required
- Quinoa, half cup
- Chai egg, one
- Fish sauce, one tablespoon
- Avocado slices, two
- Carrot slices, one cup
- Beetroot, one
- Radish, one cup
- Garlic powder, two teaspoon
- Maple syrup, half teaspoon
- Sesame oil, one teaspoon
- Salt, to taste
- Pepper, to taste

Instructions:

1. Take a large bowl and add the radishes and carrots slices into it.

2. Add the ginger and garlic powder.
3. Mix well until a good mixture is obtained.
4. Add the chai egg and quinoa into it and mix gently.
5. Add the lime juice, maple syrup and Japanese red chili.
6. Add the salt and pepper as you prefer.
7. Add the sesame oil, red bell peppers and mix well.
8. Add the pepper into the mixture for taste.
9. Add the avocado slices in the end and put the mixture on rice paper.
10. Make rolls by folding the rice papers.
11. Your dish is ready to be served.

5.6 Vietnamese Pickled Bitter Melon Salad Recipe

Preparation Time: 10 minutes
Cooking Time: 30 minutes
Serving: 2

Ingredients:

- Maple syrup, one teaspoon
- Ground ginger, a quarter teaspoon
- Picked bitter melon, two cups
- Mixed nuts, two tablespoon
- Pepper, as required
- Cilantro, half cup
- Salt, a quarter teaspoon
- Soy sauce, as required
- Mint leaves, half cup
- Salad dressing, half cup

Instructions:
1. Cut the pickled melon into large pieces.
2. Mix all the ingredients along with the melon.
3. Add the salad dressing in a bowl and beat it well.
4. Drizzle the dressing on top of the melon mixture.
5. Your dish is ready to be served.

5.7 Vietnamese Spring Rolls Recipe

Preparation Time: 40 minutes
Cooking Time: 10 minutes
Serving: 2

Ingredients:

- Rice vermicelli, one pound
- Rice wrappers, five
- Shrimp, half pound
- Fresh Thai basil, half teaspoon
- Water, one cup
- Lime juice, one tablespoon
- White sugar, two tablespoon
- Hoisin Sauce, two teaspoon
- Chopped peanuts, one tablespoon
- Garlic chili sauce, half tablespoon
- Minced garlic, one teaspoon
- Oil, for frying

Instructions:
1. Take a saucepan and add the water in it.
2. Boil the water then add the rice vermicelli.
3. Boil it and drain it after five minutes.
4. Take boiling water in large bowl.

5. Dip the wrapper into it.
6. Lay the wrapper flat and add the shrimp on top of the wrapper.
7. Add the rice vermicelli, basil and mint on top.
8. Add the lettuce and cilantro on it.
9. Roll the wrapper tightly and make sure that there is no hole in the roll.
10. Deep fry the rolls.
11. Dish out the rolls when they turn golden brown.
12. Mix the water, hoisin sauce, peanuts, garlic, lime juice and sugar to make a sauce.
13. Drizzle the sauce on top of the spring rolls or serve it along the rolls.
14. Your dish is ready to be served.

5.8 Vietnamese Chicken Baguettes Recipe

Preparation Time: 10 minutes
Cooking Time: 30 minutes
Serving: 6

Ingredients:

- Chicken, one pound
- Olive oil, one teaspoon
- Rice vinegar, one teaspoon
- Golden sugar, half tablespoon
- Spring onions, two
- Carrot, half
- Lime juice, one tablespoon
- Cucumber, two
- Baguette bread, as required
- Sweet chili sauce, one tablespoon

* Gem lettuce leaves, three
* Red chili, half teaspoon

Instructions:
1. Take a pan and add the olive oil in it.
2. Heat it and cook the chicken in it for two minutes.
3. Mix the rice vinegar and sugar and lime juice in the pan.
4. Add more sugar if needed.
5. Add the carrot, spring onions and cucumber in it.
6. Add chili per taste.
7. Split the sandwich baguette completely.
8. Stuff it with the gem leaves.
9. Add the chicken mixture on top.
10. Cover the chicken with the bread slice and toast your sandwich.
11. Serve the dish with chili sauce.

5.9 Vietnamese Fish Sauce Recipe

Preparation Time: 5 minutes
Cooking Time: 10 minutes
Serving: 4

Ingredients:

* Water, five tablespoon

- Sugar two tablespoon
- Minced garlic, one teaspoon
- Lemon juice, two tablespoon
- Fish sauce, two tablespoon

Instructions:
1. Take a bowl and add the water in it.
2. Add the sugar into it and dissolve it well.
3. Heat the water on low heat.
4. Add the lemon juice as required.
5. Then in the end, add the fish sauce.
6. Top it with the garlic and chilies.
7. Your dish is ready to be served.

5.10 Vietnamese Shrimp Tacos Recipe

Preparation Time: 30 minutes
Cooking Time: 30 minutes
Serving: 4

Ingredients:

For slaw:
- Sour cream, half cup
- Mayonnaise, a quarter cup
- Lime juice, a quarter teaspoon

- Flour, one cup
- Red onion, one cup
- Chopped cilantro, one tablespoon
- Flour tortillas, five
- Tomato salsa, half cup
- Broccoli, half cup

For the filling:

- Sugar, half cup
- Canola oil, half cup
- Shrimp, one pound
- Lime zest, a pinch
- Cumin, half teaspoon
- Chili Powder, one tablespoon
- Garlic powder, one teaspoon
- Onion powder, one teaspoon
- Dried oregano, half teaspoon
- Salt, half teaspoon

Instructions:

1. Take a large bowl and add the canola oil into it.
2. Add the sugar and salt as required.
3. Add the garlic powder and onion powder into it.
4. Add the cumin and lime zest in the same bowl
5. Mix them all thoroughly.
6. Then coat the shrimp into it and refrigerate it for thirty minutes.
7. Make slaw in a bowl by adding mayonnaise and sour cream.
8. Add the broccoli, chili and cilantro into it.
9. Mix well and season with salt.
10. Cover it and refrigerate.

11.   Wrap the tortillas in foil and bake for ten minutes.

12.   Cook the shrimps for three to five minutes.

13.   Divide the shrimps among tortillas, top with slaw.

14.   Your dish is ready to be served.

Conclusion

With a solid Chinese impact in large numbers of the dishes, the Vietnamese food is fragrant and brimming with flavor. In the last few years, Vietnamese food has gotten increasingly more well-known throughout the world. Foodies may have attempted the two most popular Vietnamese dishes: spring rolls and bread rolls. Rice, noodles, vegetables and spices all have a huge part in Vietnamese food, making it one of the best cooking in the world.

In Vietnam, you will find one undeniable truth which is that the Vietnamese love eating noodles a lot. They eat them consistently, sometimes for each supper. Vietnamese noodles are produced using a couple of fundamental ingredients, the most well-known being rice, wheat and mung beans.

Vietnamese food is not only quite unlike any other food in Southeast Asia but also regarded as one of the healthiest cuisines all over the world. Tasting Vietnamese delicious foods, tourists have chance to enjoy its uniqueness through five senses: food arrangement appealing to eyes, sounds coming from crisp ingredients, five spices lingering on the tongue, aromatic ingredients from herbs attracting the nose and some food merely being perceived by touching.

This book covers the variety of Vietnamese dishes, making it easy for the readers to prepare their favourite recipes in their kitchen without any stress. This cookbook incorporates 70 healthy plans that contain Vietnamese breakfast recipes, Vietnamese lunch and dinner recipes, Vietnamese snack recipes and Vietnamese dessert recipes that you can undoubtedly make at home very easily. So, start cooking today with this amazing and easy cookbook.

INDIAN
COOKBOOK

70 Easy Recipes for
Traditional Food from
India

Maki Blanc

© Copyright 2021 by Maki Blanc - All rights reserved.

This document is geared towards providing exact and reliable information in regard to the topic and issue covered. The publication is sold with the idea that the publisher is not required to render accounting, officially permitted, or otherwise, qualified services. If advice is necessary, legal or professional, a practiced individual in the profession should be ordered.

- From a Declaration of Principles which was accepted and approved equally by a Committee of the American Bar Association and a Committee of Publishers and Associations.

It is not legal in any way to reproduce, duplicate, or transmit any part of this document in either electronic means or in printed format. Recording of this publication is strictly prohibited and any storage of this document is not allowed unless with written permission from the publisher. All rights reserved.

The information provided herein is stated to be truthful and consistent, in that any liability, in terms of inattention or otherwise, by any usage or abuse of any policies, processes, or directions contained within is the solitary and utter responsibility of the recipient reader. Under no circumstances will any legal responsibility or blame be held against the publisher for any reparation, damages, or monetary loss due to the information herein, either directly or indirectly.

Respective authors own all copyrights not held by the publisher.

The information herein is offered for informational purposes solely and is universal as so. The presentation of the information is without contract or any type of guarantee assurance.

The trademarks that are used are without any consent, and the publication of the trademark is without permission or backing by the trademark owner. All trademarks and brands within this book are for clarifying purposes only and are the owned by the owners themselves, not affiliated with this document.

Introduction

Seasoning blends, heady herbs, and bright colors prevail in Indian cuisine, aromatic and tasty. It also contains anti-inflammatory micronutrients in abundance. If Indian cuisine is unfamiliar to you, it can seem intimidating, but do not worry: these dishes describe in the book are surprisingly simple to prepare. Indeed, once you have had a few culinary triumphs, you might choose to create Indian-influenced dishes, a frequent part of your culinary range. Fragrant spices, which are a staple of Indian cuisine, are better when used fresh. You will save money by purchasing fresh spices in limited amounts from your nearest natural foods market's bulk section.

In terms of cuisine, India can be split into four distinct regions. Each area contains numerous nations, each with its distinct cuisine. Here is a quick rundown of North, East, South, and West Indian delicacies. Of course, it is important to keep in mind that no single explanation can encompass the vast array of Indian cuisine. It can take years of meticulous and really enjoyable gastronomic exploration to discover it.

Indian cuisine offers a wide variety of flavors, both strong and subtle, that is as diverse as the country itself. Weather and elevation, as well as culture and faith, both have an impact on the area. They describe a broad range of cuisines, which is unsurprising in a world with an estimated 885 million people and a land area of 1,226,596 square miles. Aside from herbs' prominent use, flatbreads and much larger milk products than anywhere in Asia are traditional culinary threads that run through local cuisines. Based on the region, baked goods are made from wheat, rice, or ground vegetables, while processed foods include milk, cream, yogurt, heavy cream, cream cheese, and cheese.

Religion has unquestionably had the greatest impact on Indian cuisine. Centuries of Hindu tradition and a deep conviction in reincarnation have culminated in some of the world's most delectable vegetarian food. Vegans rely on a variety of whole and split vegetables for nutrition. They have a wholesome, diverse diet combined with grain, supported by vegetables and milk products, and flavored to the full. Indian cuisine is similar to defining European cuisine in that it encompasses all at once.

"Indian Cookbook" is a complete recipe book based on all types of Indian dishes. It has four chapters with detailed knowledge of the introduction to Indian cuisine. Recipes from different regions of India are given in each chapter. These chapters are characterized into breakfast, appetizers, snacks, lunch, dinner, desserts, soups, salad, and India's most famous dishes. Try these dishes at your home and make your meals more like Indians.

Chapter 1: Introduction to Indian Cuisine

Food and drink are considered to nourish both the soul and the skin in India; food is central to spiritual development, pleasure, and happiness. The Indian kitchen differs greatly from north to eastern side to south, with western and southern Indian curries leading the way to vegan Indian food since most Western people recognize and enjoy it.

A cook's ingenuity and situations are the only limits to the richness of Indian cuisine. Each Indian chef, rest assured, would be a master of seasoning, handling each one separately before mixing them into different masalas (spice blends). Indians, like foreigners, are passionate about their cuisine. Three meals per day are normal, but certain areas of the country are so impoverished that they can only manage one. More than 500 million Indians, out of a total population of 1.2 billion, survive on less than $2.50 per day. However, whoever can enjoy their three primary meals and pack as many tiffins (snack foods) as they can into their everyday diet without sabotaging their hunger.

1.1 History of Indian Cuisine

Ayurveda, the ancient philosophy of life, fitness, and immortality, has influenced modern Indian culinary traditions. Foods are classified in Ayurveda based on their positive and negative forces and medicinal benefits. It is now the most commonly practiced treatment system in India, established by the Aryans in the second millennium BC. The fundamental theory of 'you are what you consume – you consume accordingly to what you are' is that you cannot sustain a balanced body by eating inappropriate food.

Much of this has not prevented fast-food franchises from establishing themselves in India's megacities like Mumbai, Delhi, and Calcutta. However, the ordinary Indian will still choose home-cooked food and a nearby ayurvedic practitioner to everything else. Moreover, although meat (except beef) is not specifically forbidden in Hinduism, a number of Indians are vegetarians due to the close connection between moral purity and veganism. Ahimsa (non-injury) is a Hindu and Jains ideology, but Buddhism has a much less humane perspective and is more concerned with intellectual development than animal health.

Such foods are considered pure and holy, and they can be used in temple rituals. The Hindu pantheon has a favorite dish; Krishna, for example, enjoys dairy goods, while Ganesha is often represented with a bowl of modak. Prasad is any meal that is first given to the deities and then exchanged with others.

1.2 History of Traditional Dishes of Indian Food

Indians are voracious consumers of home-cooked food or something done in the privacy of their own homes. The idea of dining in cafes and a posh Indian restaurant tradition has only been around for around fifty years. The Indian side of the road restaurants known as Dhaba is more like a lifestyle – an oasis for truckers, bus riders, and tourists going anywhere by the highway in India's vast, scenic, and often demanding landscape are as common as residence food. India's traditional dishes have roots in the Muslim-Indian era.

Indians are passionate about their food. Cooking is regarded as an art form, and moms often begin teaching their girls and passing down traditional foods by show-and-tell when their daughters are young. Mealtimes are significant moments for family gatherings. The majority of meals consist of many dishes ranging from basics such as rice and bread to meat and veg, followed by a dessert. Food is prepared from home with quality ingredients in many Indian families. Instead of buying grain from a supermarket, some families buy their favorite kind of grain, wash it, drying it in the heat, and then bring it to a factory to have it processed into flour just the way they like it! This is happening in larger cities, where people are happier to use ready-to-eat, pre-made foods because their lives are becoming more hectic.

1.3 Nutritional Information and Benefits of Indian Food

There are many benefits of Indian cuisine.
Chickpeas, for instance, which are frequently used in vegan curries, are high in fiber, calcium, riboflavin, and phosphorus, making them a nutritious addition to a vegan Indian diet. Superfoods such as broccoli and carrots, commonly used in Indian cuisine, produce rich antioxidants, nutrients, and minerals. Most Indian sauces and toppings, like Sag aloo and Gobhi Aloo (cabbage with vegetables), are veggies, making them a healthier option because they do not use milk or dairy. The tangy yogurt dipping raita, made with natural milk, tomato, and mint, is a low-fat option to sauces like mayonnaise and is a source of nutrients. In place of milk or cocoa powder, natural porridge is sometimes used to make curry preserves.

Garlic, which would be good for health, and cloves, which are great for the immune response and digestion, are commonly used in Indian cuisine. Instead of butter, Indian dishes frequently use grain, red pepper, and rice flour, maintaining the saturated fat content. Finally, since Indian dishes have such a strong flavor, a limited portion may also please taste buds while consuming fewer calories. The versatility and vibrancy of an Indian diet make it exciting, which is a good aspect of any cuisine because variety prevents repetition and overeating.

Finally, choosing tandoori recipes will reduce fat and calorie intake since they have very few sauces, and the meal, which is usually poultry and seafood, is grilled rather than fried.

Mango, bananas, pomegranates, figs, tomatoes, strawberries, grapefruit, oranges, and guavas are among the many delights of an Indian diet be consumed regularly to aid digestion and acquire minerals and vitamins.

1.4 Key ingredients of Indian Food

Here are some of the most important spices in Indian cooking.

Garam Masala: Garam means "hot" or "warm" in Hindi, and this mix of chilly spices from northwestern India's cooler climates brings a sense of heat both to the mouth and the soul.

Fenugreek: This herbal tree is found for its surprisingly bitter, somewhat sweet leaves, rich and round with a mild crunch.

Cinnamon's flavor and scent are distinctively woody, stinky, and velvety, and it has a warming effect on the palate.

Coconuts: Coconut milk and oils are essential in Northern Indian cooking, commonly used in curries.

Cumin has a distinct musty, earthy taste with some yellowish notes, making it an essential component in garam masala and chili powder.

Mint: This calming herb has a surprisingly fresh, herbal, sweet taste that goes well with lamb recipes and is used in raitas and curries.

Cardamom is a spice that is used in cooking. Cardamom has a lime, herbal, soapy taste with some bright yellow notes, making it an essential spice in garam masala.

Turmeric is a dried powdered root with a musky, oaky scent and a peppery, mildly bitter taste.

Chiles are native to South America and were brought to India by the Dutch.

Tamarind: Also known as Indian date, condensed tamarind paste is used to give curries and sauces a sour taste.

Cloves have a heavy, pungent, soft, almost spicy taste.

Cilantro: Cilantro (clean cilantro) has a waxy, citrusy, and soapy taste and fragrance.

Chapter 2: Indian Appetizers Recipes

2.1 Nippattu

Cooking Time: 30 minutes
Serving Size: 15-20
Ingredients:
- ¼ cup water or less
- Oil for frying
- ¾ teaspoon salt or as required
- 2 tablespoon hot oil
- 2 sprigs curry leaves
- 1 teaspoon red chili powder
- 1 cup rice flour
- 2 tablespoon dry coconut
- 1 tablespoon sesame seeds
- 2 tablespoon all-purpose flour
- ¼ cup peanuts
- 3 tablespoon fried gram
- 2 tablespoon chiroti rava

Method:
1. Dry roast groundnuts in a skillet until the skin begins to peel.
2. Add the dry coconut and bake for 20-30 seconds with the groundnut.
3. In a machine, combine all of the ingredients.
4. Set that aside after pulsing it into a gritty powder.
5. Add rice flour to the same pot and dry bake for two minutes on medium heat.
6. Insert the all-purpose starch and rava, and proceed to roast for 1 minute more.

7. Merge fine groundnut dust, dried chili powder, minced curry leaves, green onions, and salts in this roast rice flour.
8. Add the oil for frying over medium-high heat.
9. Pick the rolled pastry and gently place it in the hot oil.
10. Take the fried nippattu out of the oil and serve.

2.2 Thattai

Cooking Time: 40 minutes
Serving Size: 25 thattai

Ingredients:
For Roasting
- 1 cup rice flour
- 1 tablespoon urad dal

Other Ingredients
- 10 tablespoons water
- Oil as required
- ½ teaspoon red chili powder
- 2 tablespoons coconut
- ½ teaspoon salt
- 1 teaspoon white sesame seeds
- 1 tablespoon chana dal
- ¼ teaspoon asafoetida powder
- 1 tablespoon chana dal
- 1 tablespoon curry leaves
- 1 tablespoon butter

Method:
1. Wash the chana dal and keep it in hot water for a few minutes.
2. A hardpan should be heated. Toss in the urad dal.
3. For 2 minutes, gently roast the urad dal.
4. Add rice flour to the same plate.

5. Fry the corn starch on moderate to medium heat, often moving, until it is soft to the touch.
6. Keep the roasted urad dal and grind it in a small mixer.
7. Add roasted chana dal as well.
8. Combine the rest of the ingredients, as well as the spices.
9. Mix the butter and flour with your fingertips.
10. To make a semi-soft dough, combine all ingredients and knead until smooth.
11. In a skillet, keep oil for slow cooking.
12. Shape the dough into little balls.
13. Put softly in the hot oil.
14. Start frying the thattai on medium heat.
15. Fry the thattai until it is crisp and golden brown.

2.3 Shankarpali

Cooking Time: 1 hour
Serving Size: 1 jar

Ingredients:

- 3 to 3.5 tablespoon milk
- 2 tablespoon ghee
- ½ cup regular sugar
- 1 pinch salt
- ½ cup Rava
- 1.5 cups all-purpose flour

Method:

1. In a dry mixer, dust the sugar and set it aside.
2. To begin, salt the flour and sieve it.
3. The crushed sugar should then be sieved.
4. The oil should be warm.
5. Make a breadcrumb-like texture by mixing the fat into the flour mix.

6. Heat the milk in the microwave.
7. Then, one tablespoon at a time, insert the hot milk and whisk to a strong, tight mixture.
8. Cover and set aside for thirty minutes.
9. In a skillet, heat the oil for slow cooking.
10. Divide the dough into two parts is a good idea.
11. Transfer 8 of these cuts into the pan softly.
12. If you have a larger skillet, you can cook more.
13. Fry the shankarpali until golden brown.
14. Create diamond-shaped pieces out of the other slice of dough in the same way.
15. Fry such cuts too in quantities and serve.

2.4 Namak Para

Cooking Time: 1 hour 5 minutes
Serving Size: 4

Ingredients:
- Salt to taste
- Oil for frying
- 2 to 3 tablespoon oil
- ½ to ¾ cup water
- 1 teaspoon cumin seeds
- ¼ teaspoon baking soda
- 1 teaspoon carom seeds
- 1 teaspoon black pepper
- 1 cup all-purpose flour
- 1 cup wheat flour

Method:
1. Combine the whole wheat grain, wheat bread, white vinegar, and salt in a large mixing bowl.

2. Carom seeds can be included now.
3. Combine the carom seeds and the remaining sieved flours.
4. Start kneading the dough with the water.
5. Shape the dough into medium-sized spheres and roll them in flour.
6. Create criss-cross shapes on the rolling dough with a sharp blade.
7. Take the diamond-shaped designs from the skillet and pan-fry them in hot oil until lightly browned and crispy.
8. When they have cooled down, place them in an airtight container.
9. Namak para can be served with tea or as a snack.

2.5 Jhal Muri

Cooking Time: 15 minutes
Serving Size: 3

Ingredients:
Main Ingredients

- 1 teaspoon lemon juice
- 2 tablespoons coconut
- 1 teaspoon mustard oil
- 3 tablespoons coriander leaves
- 2 cups puffed rice
- ¼ cup roasted peanuts
- 3 tablespoons chana chur
- ¼ cup onions
- 1 to 2 green chilies
- ½ teaspoon ginger
- ¼ cup tomato
- ½ cup boiled potatoes
- ¼ cup cucumber

Spice Powders

- ½ teaspoon black salt

- ½ teaspoon rock salt
- ¼ teaspoon garam masala powder
- 1 teaspoon mango powder
- ½ teaspoon coriander powder
- ¼ teaspoon black pepper
- ½ teaspoon red chili powder
- ½ teaspoon cumin powder

Method:

1. To begin, finely chop the vegetables.
2. Set them aside for now.
3. Heat a wok over moderate to medium heat.
4. Put two cups of puffed rice into the mixture.
5. Turn off the heat and place the pan on the counter.
6. The fire from the skillet will roast and aromatize the spice powders.
7. Combine the puffed rice and seasoning powders in a mixing bowl.
8. Add ¼ cup roasted peanuts to the mix.
9. The coarsely diced onions, peppers, mushrooms, diced peppers, and ginger are then added.
10. After that, squirt one teaspoon of lime juice all over.
11. Re-blend gently.
12. Add sev to the mixture. You may also use chana chur rather than sev.
13. Coriander leaf should be added at this stage.
14. Taste and season with more salt, lime juice, or seasoning powders if desired.
15. Jhal muri should be served right away.

2.6 Spring Rolls

Cooking Time: 1 hour
Serving Size: 3
Ingredients:
Filling

- 1½ tablespoon oyster sauce
- 2 teaspoon soy sauce
- 1½ cups green cabbage
- 1 teaspoon cornflour
- 1½ cups carrot
- 1½ cups bean sprouts
- 1 tablespoon oil
- 400g pork
- 6 shiitake mushrooms
- 2 garlic cloves

Spring Rolls

- 1 tablespoon water
- Oil for frying
- 2 teaspoon cornflour
- 20 spring roll wrappers

Sweet and Sour Sauce

- 2 tablespoon tomato ketchup
- 2 teaspoon soy sauce
- ½ cup apple cider vinegar
- 1/3 cup brown sugar
- 2 tablespoon water
- 2 teaspoon cornflour

Method:

1. In a pan or wok, melt the oil over medium temperature.

2. Insert the garlic and whisk rapidly before adding the bacon.
3. Carrots, bean sprouts, lettuce, and mushrooms are all good additions.
4. Cook for three minutes until it has ripened veggies.
5. Cook for two minutes, or until the liquid has evaporated, adding cornflour, sesame oil, and oyster sauce as needed.
6. In a small bowl, combine cornstarch and water.
7. Fill a skillet or big saucepan halfway with oil to twice the height of the spring rolls.
8. Heat on high for a few minutes before hot.
9. Put spring rolls in the oils and fry, turning regularly, for two minutes, or until deep yellow. Repeat for the rest of the spring rolls.
10. Offer with Sweet and Tamarind Chutney while it is still hot!

2.7 Punugulu

Cooking Time: 30 minutes
Serving Size: 2-3

Ingredients:
- Salt as required
- Oil for deep frying
- 3 teaspoon coriander leaves
- 1 teaspoon cumin seeds
- ½ inch ginger
- 1 or 2 green chilies
- 1 cup idli batter
- 1 small onion
- 6 curry leaves
- 1 tablespoon rava

Method:

1. In a mixing dish, combine 1 cup idli mixture or dosa mixture.
2. Insert two to three teaspoon cilantro leaves, chopped garlic, Rava, cabbage, chopped cabbage, curry leaf, sliced mustard seeds, garlic, green chilies, two to three teaspoon cardamom leaves.
3. In a wok or skillet, heat the oil for slow cooking.
4. The exterior should be smooth, while the interior should be warm and plush.
5. If the mixture is too thick, a few teaspoons of water should be added.
6. In moderate oil, drop tablespoons of the batter.
7. Turn over until the sides are pale golden, and clear.
8. Fry them in medium-high heat, rotating them a few times to ensure even browning.
9. Punugulu is best served hot or warm with almond or nut chutney.

2.8 Vegetable Cutlets

Cooking Time: 45 minutes
Serving Size: 3

Ingredients:

- ⅓ cup bread crumbs
- 3 tablespoons oil
- 2 tablespoons all-purpose flour
- 3 tablespoons water
- ½ cup boiled carrots
- ½ teaspoon masala powder
- 3 tablespoons bread crumbs
- 1 cup boiled potatoes
- ¼ teaspoon red chili powder
- ½ teaspoon cumin powder
- ½ inch ginger

- ½ cup fresh green peas

Method:
1. In a broiler pan or heat cooker, thoroughly cook the potato, cabbage, and green peas.
2. When the vegetables are cooling, finely chop four to five slices of toast in a mixing bowl or blender to make bread crumbs.
3. Set aside the bread crumbs on a sheet or plate.
4. Slice and cut the carrots and potatoes.
5. Use a spoon or a masher to smash them.
6. Mix with the rest of the ingredients.
7. Add two tablespoon all-purpose starch and three tablespoon liquid in a separate small bowl.
8. Put the cutlet combination on a plate, then.
9. In a skillet, heat two to three tablespoons of oil for deep frying.
10. Then thinly roll the cutlet in breadcrumbs.
11. Remove any leftover bread crumbs before placing them in the medium-hot liquid.
12. Flip a few more times to ensure that all of the vegetables are cooked through.

Chapter 3: Indian Breakfast Recipes

3.1 Soft Idli

Cooking Time: 9 hours 25 minutes
Serving Size: 30 idli

Ingredients:
- 1 teaspoon rock salt
- Oil as required
- ¼ teaspoon fenugreek seeds
- Water
- ½ cup whole urad dal
- ¼ cup thick poha
- 1 cup regular rice

Method:
1. Both normal and preboiled rice should be picked and rinsed.
2. Fill the container halfway with water.
3. Individually soak the urad dal and methi seeds in liquid for five hours.
4. Drain the urad dal that has been soaked.
5. For a few seconds, grind the urad dal, methi seed, and ¼ cup of the allocated water.
6. Then pour in the remaining ¼ cup of water. Grind until the batter is thick and moist.
7. To form a delicious batter, ground the rice in quantities.
8. Grease the idli molds and set them aside.
9. In a slow cooker or hotplate, pour the mixture into the molds and steam the idli.
10. Heat for 15 to 20 minutes, or until the idlis are cooked through.

11.   Offer the hot steaming idli with sambar and mango chutney.

3.2 Crispy Dosa

Cooking Time: 14 hours
Serving Size: 15 dosa
Ingredients:
Dosa Batter

- 1 teaspoon rock salt
- Ghee or oil
- ½ teaspoon methi seeds
- 3 tablespoons flattened rice
- 1 tablespoon chana dal
- 1 tablespoon toor dal
- ¾ cup idli rice
- ½ cup urad dal gota
- ¾ cup Sona masoori rice

Potato Masala

- ½ teaspoon salt
- Cilantro to garnish
- 15 curry leaves
- ½ teaspoon turmeric powder
- 4 medium potatoes
- 1 medium onion
- 1-2 green chilies
- 6 cashews broken
- 1 teaspoon ginger
- 1 tablespoon oil
- ¼ teaspoon asafoetida
- 1 teaspoon chana dal
- ½ teaspoon mustard seeds

Method:

1. Transfer sona masoori grain, toor dal, urad dal gota, and methi seeds, in a big mixing cup.
2. Pour the water from the grain, dals, and poha before blending it in a high-powered blender.
3. Now, pass the mixture to the Instant Pot's steel pan.
4. One teaspoon rock salt can be added to the mixture.
5. Pour the salt into the mixture for two minutes with your hands.
6. In a medium-sized tub, heat one tablespoon of oil.
7. Toss in the chana dal, cashew nuts, and spice, minced.
8. Add the chopped onion, diced peppers, and coriander seeds after that.
9. Cook for about two minutes, or until the vegetables are softened.
10. Add the cinnamon and pepper to the boiling and whipped potatoes.
11. On medium-high fire, heat a cast iron pan.
12. Cut an onion in half, pierce it with a blade, and then drop it in oil.
13. Then begin preparing the dosa. Fill a ladle halfway with batter and dump it into the pan's middle.
14. Drizzle peanut oil or butter all over the dosa, as well as in the middle.
15. Fold in the cooked potato masala.
16. Prepare all of the dosas in the same manner.
17. Serve fried masala dosas immediately with sambar, coriander coconut lime pickle, or tomatillo salsa.

3.3 Uttapam

Cooking Time: 40 minutes
Serving Size: 8
Ingredients:
  - 1 teaspoon kosher salt
  - ¼ cup water
  - 4 cups Idli Batter

Toppings
  - ½ cup cilantro
  - ¼ cup ghee
  - 2 tomatoes
  - 2 to 4 green chilies
  - 1 medium red onion

Method:
1. To make a pancake-like texture, add salt and sugar to the idli batter.
2. To make a 6-inch croissant, spread around two spoons full of batter.
3. First, on the uttapam, place one tablespoon onions, pepper, ¼ teaspoon green chili, and ½ tablespoon coriander.
4. With a small silicone spoon, gently pick up the uttapam, coming in from the sides and touching the middle, and turn it over.
5. As the onions begin to caramelize, fry the strong part for 1 to 2 minutes.
6. Remove the uttapam and eat with mango pickle or cilantro leaf chutney and paratha, top side up.
7. Repeat for the rest of the batter.

3.4 Pesarattu

Cooking Time: 4 hours 20 minutes
Serving Size: 7

Ingredients:
For Batter

- 1 tablespoon rice flour
- Salt to taste
- 2 tablespoon chana dal
- Water as required
- 1 cup moong dal

Other Ingredients

- 1-inch ginger
- 1 green chili
- Half onion
- Seven teaspoon oil

Method:

1. First, soak chana dal and mong dal for at minimum up to eight hours in a big mixing cup.
2. Drain the water and mix the batter until it is creamy.
3. Place in a big mixing cup.
4. To put additional crispiness, add corn starch.
5. Season with salt to taste.
6. Shake the batter thoroughly until it reaches the strength of the dosa batter.
7. Using a spoon, spill a ladleful of batter onto a frying pan.
8. Place it thinly in a clockwise direction.
9. Over the pessarattu, spread a little coarsely diced onions, jeera, chili - pepper, and oil.
10. Strip the dosa from the ends gradually.
11. And then fold it into a triangle or some other shape you like.
12. Serve pessarattu with warm uppitu, allam sorbet, or mango pickle as a finishing touch.

3.5 Egg Toast

Cooking Time: 1 toast
Serving Size: 30 minutes

Ingredients:

- Salt, to taste
- Pepper, to taste
- 1 egg
- 3 tablespoons shredded cheese
- ½ tablespoon butter
- 1 slice bread

Method:

1. To make a bowl, press it down on the middle of the loaf with a spoon.
2. Spread the butter around the sides of the loaf and crack the egg into the jar.
3. Spread melted cheese along the bread's sides.
4. Season with salt and pepper and cook for fifteen minutes at 400°F.
5. A runny yolk will result after ten minutes, while a firmer yolk will result after fifteen minutes.

3.6 Egg Paratha

Cooking Time: 30 minutes
Serving Size: 2

Ingredients:

- 2 tablespoon coriander leaves
- ½ teaspoon garam masala
- ¼ cup onions
- 1 green chili
- 2 cups whole wheat flour
- 1 tablespoon oil
- 2 eggs
- A pinch of salt

Method:

1. Add flour, pepper, and oils to a measuring bowl, and whisk the combination into a flat dough with 1 cup of water.
2. If the flour seems to be dry, apply a little more liquid. Knead thoroughly.
3. Make four balls out of the dough.
4. Whisk together the eggs, carrots, chili, coriander, curry powder, and salt in a mixing cup. Set aside for now.
5. Put the rolled pastry on a frying pan and bake on both sides for 1-2 minutes.
6. Cook for another minute after adding a little oil to the surface.
7. Create a slit as soon as the edges begin to crisp.
8. More oil should be drizzled on the paratha, and the layer should be softly pressed with the back of the knife.

3.7 Egg Mayo Sandwich

Cooking Time: 35 minutes
Serving Size: 4

Ingredients:

- Salt and pepper to taste
- ¼ teaspoon paprika
- 1 teaspoon yellow mustard
- ¼ cup green onion
- ½ cup mayonnaise
- 8 eggs

Method:

1. In a frying pan, crack the egg and coat it with ice water.
2. Bring the water to a boil and then remove it from the heat.
3. Allow eggs to sit in hot water for 10 - 15 minutes, covered.
4. Take from the hot water, allow to cool before peeling and slicing.
5. In a mixing dish, combine the diced eggs, mayo, vinegar, and spring onions.
6. Season with parmesan, lime, and pepper.
7. Combine all ingredients in a mixing bowl and serve with your choice of bread or crackers.

Chapter 4: Indian Snack Recipes

4.1 Vegetable Pakora

Cooking Time: 20 minutes
Serving Size: 5
Ingredients:
Ketchup Chutney

- ½ teaspoon sugar
- ½ teaspoon salt
- 1 tablespoon water
- ½ tablespoon chaat masala
- ½ cup ketchup

Pakora Batter

- 1 cup luke-warm water
- Sunflower oil
- ½ cup cilantro leaves
- 1 yellow onion
- 2 cups besan
- ½ teaspoon baking powder
- 1 green chili pepper
- ¾ teaspoon sea salt
- 1 tablespoon red pepper flakes

Method:

1. In a mixing dish, combine all of the chutney components.
2. Half-fill an 8-inch cast-iron pan or other heavy-bottom pot with grease.
3. Preheat the oil to 375 degrees Fahrenheit.
4. Combine the besan, dried chili flakes, flour, icing sugar, sliced chili pepper, coriander, and diced onion in a big mixing cup.

5. Slowly drizzle in the water, constantly stirring with a spoon or your fingers.
6. When the oil is hot enough, gently drop a heaping tablespoon of mixture into it.
7. Fry the pakoras until they are a pecan-brown color.
8. Then use a cooling rack over a baking sheet, clean the pakoras.
9. Continue for the remaining hitter.
10. Serve the hot pakoras with the Tomato sauce Chutney straight away.

4.2 Onion Pakoras

Cooking Time: 30 minutes
Serving Size: 4

Ingredients:
- Water as required
- Salt as required
- 1 pinch baking soda
- Oil as required
- 1 teaspoon carom seeds
- 1 pinch asafoetida
- 2 medium onions
- ½ teaspoon garam masala powder
- ¼ teaspoon turmeric powder
- 1 cup gram flour
- 1 tablespoon coriander leaves
- 2 teaspoon green chilies

Method:
1. Finely chop the onions and place them in a blending dish.
2. Add the chopped green chilies as well.
3. Carom seeds, fenugreek seeds, asafoetida, and salt are added to the pan.

4. Combine all of the ingredients thoroughly.
5. Toss in the gram flour.
6. To make a moderate batter, add the appropriate volume of water.
7. With a fork or your hands, thoroughly combine the ingredients.
8. Transfer tablespoons of the flour to the hot oil.
9. Turn the pakoras over with a slotted spoon when they're almost done and begin to fry.
10. Fry them until they are crispy and fluffy.
11. Remove with a slotted spoon and wash on paper towels to extract any extra oil.
12. Slit green peppers are fried in the same oil.
13. Season the green chilies with salt and toss well.

4.3 Mysore Bonda

Cooking Time: 20 minutes
Serving Size: 4

Ingredients:

<ul>
<li>1 cup all-purpose flour</li>
<li>½ teaspoon cooking soda</li>
<li>1 cup yogurt</li>
<li>¼ cup rice flour</li>
<li>3 green chilies</li>
<li>1 tablespoon coconut pieces</li>
<li>Salt - to taste</li>
<li>1 teaspoon cumin seeds</li>
<li>1 teaspoon ginger</li>
<li>1 cup water</li>
<li>Oil - to fry</li>
</ul>

Method:

1. Combine the curd and the water in a mixing bowl. Let it aside for now.
2. In a mixing cup, combine all-purpose flour, rice flour, sugar, and soda; stir to combine, then apply buttermilk to create a vada batter texture.
3. Now add the cumin, thinly sliced coconut, diced peppers, coarsely diced ginger, and stir well. Set aside for 1 hour.
4. Heat the oil for frying, then cut the dough into small round bondas and place them in the oil to fry on low heat.
5. Once it has become a light golden hue, extract it. Serve with mango pickle on the side.

4.4 Churumuri

Cooking Time: 10 minutes
Serving Size: 2

Ingredients:

<ul>
<li>1 teaspoon lemon juice</li>
<li>¼ cup sev</li>
</ul>

- 1 green chili
- 3 tablespoons coriander leaves
- 2 cups puffed rice
- 1 small carrot
- 2 tablespoons green mango
- ¼ cup peanuts
- 1 small to medium onion
- 1 medium tomato
- 1 teaspoon red chili powder
- ¼ to ⅓ teaspoon salt
- 3 pinches black salt
- 1 tablespoon coconut oil
- 3 pinches turmeric powder

Method:

1. Vegetables should be peeled, rinsed, and finely chopped.
2. In a bowl or skillet, heat ½ tablespoon essential oils.
3. Place the puffed rice on top.
4. Puffed rice grain should be roasted until crisp and chewy.
5. Put the puffed rice in the skillet and wait two to four minutes.
6. Combine the rest of the ingredients and stir well.
7. Dress with a pinch of black salt and a pinch of common salt or salt to taste.
8. Cover the puffed rice finely with cocoa butter, peanuts, seasoning powders, and salt.
9. Add the coarsely diced vegetables, green chilies, and coriander leaves at this stage.
10. Apply the lemon juice right now.
11. Mix all in fast and serve the churumuri right away.

4.5 Crispy Corn

Cooking Time: 15 minutes
Serving Size: 3

Ingredients:

For Boiling

- 2 cup sweet corn
- 1 teaspoon salt
- 4 cup water

For Frying

- ¼ teaspoon salt
- Oil
- 1 tablespoon all-purpose flour
- ¼ teaspoon pepper powder
- ¼ cup rice flour
- ¼ cup cornflour

For Masala

- 2 tablespoon capsicum
- 2 tablespoon coriander
- ¼ teaspoon salt
- 2 tablespoon onion
- ¼ teaspoon cumin powder
- ½ teaspoon amchur
- ½ teaspoon red chili powder

Method:

1. First, bring 4 cups of water and one teaspoon of salt to a boil in a large pot.
2. Boil for a moment after adding 2 cups of sweet corn.
3. To extract excess water, extract the sweet corn.
4. ¼ cup cornflour, ¼ cup corn grits, one tablespoon all-purpose flour, ¼ teaspoon spice powder, and ¼ teaspoon salt are now added to the mixture.
5. Mix thoroughly to ensure that the flour is evenly distributed in the green beans.

6. Deep fry in hot oil while maintaining a medium fire.
7. Cook on medium heat, stirring regularly until lightly browned.
8. ½ teaspoon chili flakes, ¼ teaspoon smoked paprika, ½ teaspoon amchur, and ¼ teaspoon salt are added to the mixture.
9. Mix thoroughly to ensure that all of the spices are evenly distributed.
10. 2 tablespoon cabbage, two tablespoon purple cabbage, and two tablespoon coriander are indeed good additions.

4.6 Chakli

Cooking Time: 1 hour 10 minutes
Serving Size: 12

Ingredients:
- ½ cup water
- Oil for frying
- ¼ teaspoon turmeric
- 2 teaspoons kosher salt
- 1.5 teaspoons ajwain
- 1 tablespoon red chili powder
- 2 cups Bhajani flour
- ¼ cup water hot
- Two tablespoons sesame seeds
- ¼ cup oil

Method:
1. In a mixing pot, add the flour.
2. Add ¼ cup warm oil and ¼ cup warm water to the pan.
3. Combine the red chili powder, crow hop seeds, fenugreek, salt, and sesame seeds in a bowl. With a spoon, combine everything.

4. To make a soft pastry, gradually apply ice water and whisk the flour.
5. In a deep fryer or skillet, heat the oil over low heat.
6. In the chakli press, place the chakli disk with the circular pattern in the center.
7. Cautiously drop chakli into the hot liquid one at a time, being cautious not to overcrowd the deep fryer.
8. Turn them off one after three minutes and fry on the middle to low heat before light brown.
9. Before introducing the next amount of chakli, note to turn up the oil's heat too high.

4.7 Dahi Vada

Cooking Time: 40 minutes
Serving Size: 10

Ingredients:

- ½ teaspoon salt
- Oil for frying
- 1-inch ginger
- ¾ cup split black gram lentils
- 1 green chili pepper
- 3 tablespoon yellow lentils

Assembling Ingredients

- ¼ teaspoon red chili powder
- Cilantro leaves chopped
- 2 tablespoon cilantro chutney
- ½ teaspoon ground cumin
- ½ teaspoon sugar adjust
- ¼ cup tamarind chutney
- ¼ teaspoon salt adjust
- 2 cups yogurt chilled

Method:

1. Clean the lentils several times in a wide bowl before the water runs clear.
2. Pour the water that has been soaking in the pan.
3. In a mixer, combine the ginger, green chili pepper, cinnamon, and lentils.
4. Crush on medium to a low level until the batter is nearly flat.
5. To keep the lentil batter soft and moist, rapidly whip it.
6. In a skillet, heat the oil. Before creating the Vada's, please ensure the oil is hot.
7. Then use a spoon or an ice cream plunger, drop the batter into the oil.
8. When you lower the Vada's in the oil, use a spoon to avoid pouring oil over it.
9. Drench the vadas for about fifteen minutes in a lukewarm bath.
10. To extract extra moisture, take each vada and press down it between your palms.
11. Season the yogurt with sugar and salt and mix it.
12. In a pan, position the softened vadas.
13. The yogurt should be poured over them.
14. Spray the ground cumin powder and red chili powder over the tamarind and mint coriander chutneys.
15. Serve with a sprinkling of cilantro on top.

4.8 Dahi Kebab

Cooking Time: 12 hours 25 minutes
Serving Size: 6

Ingredients:

- 2 tablespoon cornflour
- Oil for deep frying
- ½ teaspoon pepper

- ¼ cup bread crumbs
- 2 tablespoon dry fruits
- Salt to taste
- 2 cups curd
- 1 green chili
- 2 tablespoon coriander leaves
- 1 cup paneer
- 1-inch ginger
- ½ small onion

Method:
1. To begin, make a smooth and creamy custard.
2. One cup of crushed paneer is also added.
3. Add the onion, spice, chili, coriander, and dried fruits to the mix as well.
4. Insert salt and cracked pepper to taste.
5. Make sure the paneer and hanging curd are thoroughly mixed.
6. To extract excess moisture, dust the tortillas with cornflour.
7. In a hot pan, deep-fry the patties.
8. Cook, stirring regularly, on medium heat.
9. Fry the patties or kababs until they are nicely browned.
10. Eventually, serve Dahi ke kabab with risotto or sauce made from pudina.

Chapter 5: Indian Lunch Recipes

5.1 Cauliflower Korma

Cooking Time: 1 hour 10 minutes
Serving Size: 6

Ingredients:

For the Roasted Cauliflower

- ½ teaspoon cumin
- 2 teaspoon salt
- ½ teaspoon turmeric
- ½ teaspoon coriander
- 1 tablespoon garam masala
- ½ teaspoon cinnamon
- 3 tablespoon oil
- 1½ kg cauliflower florets

For the Korma Curry

- 2 teaspoon sugar
- Salt and pepper to taste
- 2 cups stock
- 1 cup cream
- 1½ cups raw cashew nuts
- ½ teaspoon cinnamon
- 1 teaspoon chili powder
- 1 teaspoon turmeric
- ½ teaspoon cardamom
- 2 tablespoon butter
- 1 teaspoon coriander
- 1 teaspoon cumin
- 1 large onion
- 3 teaspoon crushed ginger
- 1 tablespoon garam masala
- 4 garlic cloves

Method:

1. Preheat the oven to 400 degrees Fahrenheit.
2. Mix all of the food items for the roasted cauliflower.
3. Put the cauliflower in the oven and bake for thirty minutes or until it is caramelized and crispy.
4. Meanwhile, soak the walnuts for ten minutes in hot water.
5. In the butter, cook the onion, parsley, and ginger until sticky and citrusy.
6. Cook for another minute after adding the spices.
7. Wash the cashews and blend them with the flour mixture, stock, and yogurt in a food processor.
8. Mix thoroughly, then sprinkle with salt, pepper, and sucrose in a frying pan.
9. Enable for ten minutes of gentle simmering after adding the roasted cauliflower.
10. Season with salt and pepper and serve with rice, hummus, and buttered cashews.

5.2 Chicken Madras Curry

Cooking Time: 35 minutes
Serving Size: 3-4

Ingredients:

- 400g can tomatoes
- Small pack coriander
- 1-2 teaspoon chili powder
- 4 chicken breasts
- 1 onion
- 1 teaspoon cumin
- 1 teaspoon coriander
- 2 garlic cloves
- 1 tablespoon vegetable oil
- ½ teaspoon turmeric

- ½ red chili
- 1 ginger

Method:

1. In a mixing bowl, blitz the garlic, cherry tomatoes, lime, and chili flakes until coarse paste forms.
2. In a medium skillet, warm the veggie oil, add the paste, and cook over medium heat until it is loosened.
3. Stir in the turmeric, cumin seeds, coriander seeds, and hot chili flakes, then cook for a few minutes before adding the four chicken thighs.
4. Mix everything to make sure it is all covered in the spice mixture.
5. Cook until the chicken is pale in color.
6. Pan and simmer on low heat for thirty minutes, till the chicken is soft, adding 400g diced tomatoes and a large pinch of salt.
7. Serve with rice after stirring in a tiny bag of coriander.

5.3 Ennai Kathirikai Kulambu

Cooking Time: 40 minutes
Serving Size: 4

Ingredients:

Other Ingredients

- Salt as required
- 1 teaspoon jaggery powder
- ¼ teaspoon turmeric powder
- 1 cup water
- 10 curry leaves
- 2 pinch asafoetida
- 3 tablespoons sesame oil
- ½ teaspoon mustard seeds
- 250 grams small brinjals

For Spice Paste

- ¼ teaspoon black pepper
- ⅓ cup water
- 2 teaspoons poppy seeds
- ½ teaspoon cumin seeds
- 2 dry red chilies
- 5 tablespoons fresh coconut
- 1 teaspoon urad dal
- ¼ teaspoon fenugreek seeds
- 2 teaspoons gingelly oil
- 2 teaspoons chana dal
- 1 tablespoon coriander seeds

For Tamarind Pulp

- ½ cup hot water
- 1 tablespoon tamarind

Method:

1. Heat 2 tablespoons gingelly oil in a shallow saucepan or wok and transfer 2 tablespoons chana dal.
2. Fry chana dal until light perfect, stirring frequently.
3. After that, add one teaspoon of urad dal.
4. After that, season with salt and pepper.
5. Insert two teaspoons pumpkin seeds and 14 teaspoon fenugreek
6. Add five spoonfuls of grated coconut after that.
7. Turn off the heat and place the pan on the counter.
8. To make a smooth paste, combine all of the ingredients in a blender.
9. After this, cut every brinjal in half.
10. In a skillet, heat three tablespoons of gingelly oil. 12 teaspoon tomato sauce should be added.
11. Then insert 7 to 9 curry leaves and two pinches of asafoetida into the pan.
12. Combine the brinjal and seasonings in a mixing bowl.
13. Combine the ingredients that have been prepared.
14. Serve after a final mix.

5.4 Chana Dal

Cooking Time: 1 hour
Serving Size: 4

Ingredients:

- 1 teaspoon red chile flakes
- 3 tablespoons cilantro
- 6 whole cloves
- 4 large garlic cloves
- 1 cup split chickpeas

- 1 ½ teaspoons turmeric
- 1 bay leaf
- 1 teaspoon salt
- 2 tablespoons sunflower oil
- ½ teaspoon cardamom

Method:

1. In a medium skillet, give the chana dal, fenugreek, cinnamon, lemon zest, salt, and 4 cups liquid to a boil.
2. Cook for another 20 minutes, adding 1 cup of water as needed.
3. Remove the bay leaf from the dish.
4. In a shallow dish, add the oil to start making the tadka.
5. Add the chilies to the hot oil and let them swirl for about thirty seconds until its aromatic.
6. Cook, keep stirring, till the garlic is moderate brown.
7. Spill the tadka into the dal and bring to a simmer softly.
8. Serve with coriander as a garnish.

5.5 Mughlai Biryani

Cooking Time: 1 hour 10 minutes
Serving Size: 4

Ingredients:

For Mughlai Biryani Gravy

- ½ teaspoon garam masala powder
- Salt as required
- ½ cup curd
- ⅔ cup water
- 4 tablespoon ghee
- 1 tablespoon ginger-garlic paste
- 2.5 to 3 cups veggies
- ⅓ cup green peas
- 9 black pepper
- 1 teaspoon caraway seeds
- ½ teaspoon red chili powder
- 3 green cardamoms
- 1 black cardamom
- 1-inch cinnamon
- 2 single strands of mace
- 12 almonds
- 1 tej patta
- 3 cloves
- 16 raisins
- 1 large onion
- 12 cashews

For Cooking Rice

- 5 cups water
- ½ teaspoon salt
- 3 cloves
- 3 green cardamoms
- 1.5 cups basmati rice

- 1 medium tej patta
- 2 to 3 mace
- 1-inch cinnamon

For Layering

- 2 tablespoon mint leaves
- 2 teaspoon rose water
- 3 tablespoon warm milk
- 200 grams Paneer

For White Paste

- 1 tablespoon melon seeds
- 10 to 12 almonds
- 2 tablespoon water
- 1 tablespoon coconut

Method:

1. After thirty minutes of soaking, drain the rice and set it aside.
2. 10 to 12 almonds and one tablespoon melon seeds should be soaked.
3. In a tiny grinder jar, combine them with one tablespoon of flaked coconut.
4. All of the vegetables should be rinsed, peeled, and chopped.
5. Take a pan with a thick bottom.
6. Take five cups of water and bring to a boil over high heat.
7. Now toss in the rice.
8. Cook the rice on a high heat setting.
9. Heat three to four tablespoons ghee in a slow cooker.
10. Fry the almonds, pecans, and cashew nuts.
11. Cook until the onions are golden brown and caramelized.
12. Place the cooker on the stovetop once more. Mix in the whole spice.
13. Toss in the mixed vegetables.
14. Insert the white paste that has been ground.

15.   Slow cook the veggie gravy for eight to nine minutes, stirring well.
16.   Spill half of the veggie gravy on top of the first layer.
17.   Add some paneer squares to the mix.
18.   Repeat layering with the residual veggie gravy.

5.6 Veg Pulao

Cooking Time: 50 minutes
Serving Size: 2

Ingredients:

For Pulao Masala Paste

- 1 teaspoon fennel
- ¼ cup water
- 1-inch cinnamon
- 5 cloves
- ½ cup coriander
- 2 chili
- 2 pod cardamom
- ¼ cup mint
- 2 clove garlic
- 1-inch ginger

For Veg Pulao

- 1 teaspoon salt
- 2 cup water
- ½ carrot
- ½ potato
- 2 tablespoon ghee
- ½ capsicum
- 2 tablespoon peas
- 1 tomato
- 5 beans
- 1 teaspoon cumin

- 1 bay leaf
- ½ teaspoon pepper
- 1-inch cinnamon
- 2 pod cardamom
- 3 cloves
- 5 cashew
- ½ onion
- 1 cup basmati rice

Method:

1. To begin, place whole cloves in a small blender.
2. Two tablespoon ghee, heated in a big wok, cumin, lemon zest, cloves, coriander, garlic, pepper, and cashews, are added to the pot.
3. Sauté on low heat until the spices become fragrant.
4. Put one tomato and continue to sauté.
5. Include vegetables as well.
6. Cook for a minute, just until the veggies are fragrant.
7. Please ensure the basmati rice is soaked for 20 minutes before adding the veggies.
8. The veg pulao is ready to eat after 20 minutes.

5.7 Brinjal Rice

Cooking Time: 30 minutes
Serving Size: 4

Ingredients:

- 1.5 cups basmati rice

For Ground Masala Paste

- ½ teaspoon fennel seeds
- 4 to 5 tablespoons water
- 2 cloves
- 2 green cardamoms
- 1 tablespoon coconut

- 1-inch cinnamon
- 3 tablespoons coriander leaves
- 2-inch ginger
- 7 medium garlic cloves
- 2 to 3 green chilies
- 3 tablespoons mint leaves

Other Ingredients

- ½ cup water
- Salt as required
- ¼ cup French beans
- 2 cups coconut milk
- ⅓ cup capsicum
- ⅓ cup green peas
- 3 tablespoons oil
- ⅓ cup tomatoes
- ½ to ¾ cup cauliflower florets
- 1 large tej patta
- ½ cup onions
- ½ cup carrots
- 2 cloves
- 1 green cardamom
- 1-inch cinnamon
- ½ cup potato

Method:

1. Soak 1.5 cups basmati rice in water for a few minutes.
2. Put spices in a tiny mixer jar and grind them.
3. In a 3 gallon slow cooker, heat three tablespoons of oil.
4. One-inch cloves, two garlic, and one green cinnamon can be added right away.
5. Fry spices for a few seconds before fragrant.
6. Then add a third of a cup of sliced tomatoes.
7. Now add the masala paste that has been ground.

8. After that, toss in the vegetables.
9. After that, add the rice.
10. Cook for ten minutes on medium heat in a pressure cooker.
11. With some raita, eat veg brinji grain.

5.8 Drumstick Sambar

Cooking Time: 35 minutes
Serving Size: 4

Ingredients:

For Sambar Powder

- Few curry leaves
- Pinch Hing
- 1 teaspoon chana dal
- 20 dried red chili
- 1 teaspoon coconut oil
- 1 tablespoon cumin
- ½ teaspoon methi
- ¼ cup coriander seeds
- 1 teaspoon urad dal

For Sambar

- ½ cup tamarind extract
- 2 tablespoon coriander
- 2 cup water
- 2 cup toor dal
- 3 teaspoon oil
- 1 teaspoon salt
- 20 pieces drumstick
- 1 teaspoon mustard
- 1 tomato
- ½ teaspoon turmeric
- 3 dried red chili
- Few curry leaves

- 7 shallots
- Pinch Hing

Method:
1. To begin, warm three teaspoon oil in a broad wok and splutter the tempering.
2. Sauté for two minutes with seven shallots.
3. As well, put one tomato in the pan and cook until it softens.
4. 12 teaspoon garlic, two tablespoons payasam powder, and one teaspoon salt are also added.
5. Cook for 20 minutes after adding the drumsticks.
6. Two cup toor dal and 1 cup water are now included.
7. Cover and cook over medium heat or until the flavors are completely absorbed.
8. 12 cup tamarind extract should also be added and thoroughly mixed.
9. Boil for another five minutes.
10. Finally, toss in 2 tablespoons coriander and serve with hot steamed rice.

5.9 Navratan Korma

Cooking Time: 50 minutes
Serving Size: 5
Ingredients:
- Pinch garam masala
- 2 tablespoons pineapple pieces

* 1 tablespoon pomegranate arils
* Pinch cardamom powder
* 2 onion
* 5-6 whole cashews
* Pinch saffron
* 1-inch ginger
* 4 large garlic cloves
* 1 green chili
* 20 cashews
* ¼ cup cream
* 2 teaspoons golden raisins
* 1 tablespoon poppy seeds
* One teaspoon salt or to taste
* ¾ teaspoon sugar
* 3 cups water
* ¼ teaspoon red chili powder
* ¾ cup water
* 1 teaspoon coriander powder
* ½ teaspoon cumin powder
* 1 tablespoon ghee
* 1 bay leaf
* 1 medium potato
* 1/3 cup green peas
* 1 tablespoon oil
* 2 cloves
* 1 large carrot
* 14 green beans
* 1 cup cauliflower florets
* 3 whole green cardamom

Method:

1. Insert 3 cups water, cabbage, carrot, cloves, green chili, cashews, and pumpkin seeds in a big pan.
2. Cook for 10 minutes on medium-high heat.

3. Chop all of the vegetables, keeping in mind to chop them thinly.
4. In the meantime, add cabbage, shallots, onion, beans, and beans to a boiling water pan.
5. Cook for ten minutes over medium heat.
6. One tablespoon oil, heated in a wok.
7. Add the bay leaf, garlic, and cardamom to the pot.
8. Enable the spices to cook for a few minutes.
9. Insert the rosemary powder, cilantro, and red chili powder after the mixture has cooked for five minutes.
10. Add the vegetables and stir to combine.
11. Then stir in the milk.
12. Blend in the pomegranate, roasted cashew nuts, and pecans.
13. Insert the saffron milk that has been prepared as well.

Chapter 6: Indian Dinner Recipes

6.1 Mushroom Biryani

Cooking Time: 40 minutes
Serving Size: 3

Ingredients:

- 1 cup water
- ½ teaspoon rose water
- ½ teaspoon paprika
- ¾ teaspoon salt
- ¼ cup mint
- ½ teaspoon garam masala
- 1 cup basmati rice
- ½ cup coconut milk
- ¼ cup cilantro
- 2 tablespoons oil
- 2 teaspoons ginger-garlic paste
- 10 oz. white mushrooms
- 1 bay leaf
- 1 green chili
- 15 whole cashews
- 1 teaspoon shahi jeera
- 1 medium red onion
- 3 whole cloves
- 6 black peppercorns
- 1-inch cinnamon stick
- 4 whole green cardamom

Method:

1. Wash the basmati rice till the water is clear when you begin.

2. Transfer the seasoning to the Instant Pot's sauté feature.
3. And insert the green chili, tomato, and cashew nuts.
4. Cook for 3 minutes before adding the ginger-garlic paste and continuing to cook for two minutes.
5. Heat for 2 minutes after adding the mushrooms.
6. After that, whisk in the coconut milk.
7. Add the coriander and mint, diced.
8. The garam masala, cayenne pepper, and salt are then added.
9. Add the rice, which has been rinsed and washed.
10. Open the lid on the pot.
11. Cook for five minutes on elevated heat using the manual setting.
12. With a spoon, fluff the rice after opening the lid.
13. Serve mushrooms Biryani with yogurt or raita on the side.

6.2 Bisi Bele Bath

Cooking Time: 40 minutes
Serving Size: 3

Ingredients:
Other Ingredients
- 1 cup water
- 1 tablespoon ghee
- 1 cup toor dal
- 2½ cup rice
- ½ carrot
- ½ teaspoon jaggery
- ½ onions
- 5 beans
- 1½ teaspoon salt
- ¾ cup tamarind extract

- 2 cups water
- ¼ teaspoon turmeric
- ½ potato
- 2 tablespoon peanuts
- 2 tablespoon green peas

Bisi Bele Bath Masala

- 4 teaspoon coriander seeds
- Few curry leaves
- Pinch of hing
- 1 teaspoon oil
- 12 dried red chili
- 2 teaspoon poppy seeds
- 1 teaspoon sesame seeds
- 4 teaspoon chana dal
- 4 cloves
- 2 tablespoon dry coconut
- 3 pods cardamom
- 1-inch cinnamon
- 2 teaspoon urad dal
- ¼ teaspoon methi
- ½ teaspoon pepper
- 1 teaspoon jeera

For Tempering

- Few curry leaves
- 10 whole cashew
- 1 dried red chili
- Pinch of hing
- 1 teaspoon mustard
- 2 tablespoon ghee

Method:

1. Cook the vegetables, nuts, liquid, turmeric, and salts first.
2. Add the tamarind paste, jaggery, and vegetables at this stage.
3. Cook for ten minutes at a low temperature.

4. Fried toor dal, cooked rice, and 1 cup water are added next.
5. Boil for 20 minutes with bisi Bisi bele bath curry powder.
6. Offer bisi bele bath with boondi or a combination after adding the tempering.

6.3 Paneer Butter Masala

Cooking Time: 35 minutes
Serving Size: 4

Ingredients:
Other Ingredients
- ½ teaspoon Kasuri methi
- ¼ teaspoon garam masala
- 20 cubes paneer
- 2 tablespoon coriander
- 1 teaspoon salt
- 2 tablespoon cream
- 1 cup water
- ½ teaspoon sugar
- 2 tablespoon butter
- ¼ teaspoon garam masala
- ¼ teaspoon cumin powder
- 2 pods cardamom
- ¼ teaspoon turmeric
- 1 teaspoon red chili powder
- 1 bay leaf

For Onion Tomato Paste
- 2 tomato
- 10 cashew
- 1-inch ginger
- 3 clove garlic
- 1 teaspoon oil
- 1 onion

- 1 teaspoon butter

Method:
1. To begin, melt one teaspoon oil and one teaspoon oil in a broad wok.
2. Cook until the onion, carrot, and garlic have shrunk somewhat.
3. After a minute, apply the tomato and cashews.
4. Allow cooling entirely before transferring to the blender.
5. Blend until the paste is smooth.
6. Sauté 2 cardamom seeds and 1 star anise in oil in a wok.
7. Season with herbs and seasonings.
8. Sauté until the cloves are fragrant but not burned.
9. Mix in 2 tablespoons of milk as well.
10. Now softly fold in 20 pieces of paneer.
11. Last but not least, serve paneer butter chutney with roti or hummus.

6.4 Vangi Bath

Cooking Time: 25 minutes
Serving Size: 3

Ingredients:
For Rice
- 3 cup cooked rice
- 2 tablespoon coriander
- 1 teaspoon salt
- ½ teaspoon jaggery
- ¼ teaspoon turmeric
- ½ cup tamarind extract
- 2 tablespoon oil
- 1 dried red chili
- 2 brinjal

- 2 tablespoon peanut
- Few curry leaves
- 1 teaspoon mustard
- 1 teaspoon urad dal
- 1 teaspoon chana dal
- 1 teaspoon cumin

For Vangi Bath Masala Powder

- ½ cup dry coconut
- 20 dried red chili
- 1 tablespoon cumin
- 1 teaspoon methi
- 5-inch cinnamon
- ¼ cup urad dal
- ¼ cup chana dal
- 1 teaspoon clove
- 2 teaspoon oil
- ¼ cup coriander seeds
- 5 pods cardamom
- 2 teaspoon poppy seeds
- 1 mace

Method:

1. To begin, dry roast spice, cardamom, coriander, and mace in a big skillet.
2. Dry roast pumpkin seeds in the same pan until they begin to pop up.
3. Add one teaspoon of milk, chana dal, coriander seeds, urad dal, smoked paprika, and methi in a jar.
4. In a mixer, combine the roasted ingredients.
5. Without incorporating any liquid, blend to a powder form.
6. First, heat the oil in a big wok and add the cumin, chana dal, mustard, urad dal, and peanuts.
7. On medium heat, sauté and splutter.
8. Insert a few bay leaves and one red chili pepper at this stage.

9. Put two brinjals and cook for another two minutes.
10.   Finally, toss in 2 tablespoons coriander and serve with raita.

6.5 Kashmiri Pulao

Cooking Time: 35 minutes
Serving Size: 4

Ingredients:

- ½ cup dried fruits
- 2-3 edible rose petals
- Salt to taste
- 2 tablespoon ghee
- ½ cup fresh cream
- 1 teaspoon sugar
- 2 cups basmati rice
- 1 bay leaf
- 2 cups milk
- ½ teaspoon cumin seeds
- 1 stick cinnamon
- 3 cardamom
- 3 cloves

Method:

1. Combine the milk, cream, salt, and spice in a mixing bowl.
2. Drain the rice and set it aside.
3. In a heavy skillet, melt the ghee and add the cumin seeds, cloves, black pepper, cardamom seeds, and spices.
4. When they begin to splutter, add the rice and continue cooking in the ghee.
5. Insert 12 cup water and the milk mixture
6. Bring to the boil, then reduce to low heat and cook until the chicken is finished.

7. Gently fold in the dried berries.
8. Serve warm, with rose petals on top.

6.6 Porsha Kuzhambu

Cooking Time: 45 minutes
Serving Size: 6

Ingredients:

For Coconut Paste

- ½ teaspoon cumin seeds
- 1 teaspoon raw rice
- ¼ teaspoon peppercorns
- ½ cup grated coconut
- 4 red chili
- ½ teaspoon cooking oil

Other Ingredients

- ¼ teaspoon turmeric powder
- 2 teaspoon salt
- ½ cup toor dal

Vegetables

- 1 carrot
- 1 drumstick
- 50 grams cucumber
- 50 grams elephant yam
- 2 brinjal
- 50 grams snake gourd

For Tempering

- 1 sprig of curry leaves
- ¼ teaspoon asafoetida
- 1 teaspoon mustard seeds
- 1 teaspoon split urad dal
- 1 teaspoon cooking oil

Method:

1. In a slow cooker, heat the thurdal until tender, then mash the dhal.
2. Soak the uncooked rice for a while in the water.
3. All of the veggies should be chopped into small sections.
4. Wash the raw rice in water for a few minutes.
5. Load the oil into a different pan and cook the red chilies and black peppercorns for a moment.
6. In a blender, combine the fried chilies, pepper, coconut, chopped garlic, and washed raw rice.
7. Use water, process the components into a smooth paste.
8. Finally, insert the ground mixture and get the kuzhambu to a simmer.
9. Load the oil into a different pan and add the bay leaves.
10. Now you can eat the Poritha Kuzhambu with boiled rice.

6.7 Potato Kurma

Cooking Time: 45 minutes
Serving Size: 5

Ingredients:

- 1 tablespoon sunflower oil
- Salt, as required
- 1 teaspoon coriander
- ½ teaspoon garam masala
- 3 potato
- ½ teaspoon turmeric powder
- 1- ½ teaspoon red chili
- 1 onion
- 1-inch cinnamon stick
- 1 teaspoon ginger garlic paste
- 1 bay leaf
- 2 tomatoes

Ingredients to Grind
- ½ cup fresh coconut
- 1 teaspoon cumin seeds
- 1 teaspoon fennel seeds

Method:
1. Cook the potatoes in the pressure cooker.
2. In a blender, combine all of the ingredients listed under "To Grinding" and crush them into a thick powder.
3. In a medium deep fryer, heat the oil.
4. Cinnamon, garlic, bay leaf, and coarsely diced onion are added to the pot.
5. Sauté for several minutes with the ginger garlic paste.
6. Heat until the vegetables have broken down into a sauce.
7. Heat until the cayenne pepper, dried chili powder, balsamic vinegar, and curry paste powder are mixed with the onion-tomato mixture.
8. Transfer the thinly sliced potatoes to the bowl and mix them well with the spicy combination. Serve immediately.

6.8 Matar Paneer

Cooking Time: 10 minutes
Serving Size: 2
Ingredients:
- Small pack coriander
- Naan bread, roti, or rice
- 150g frozen peas

- 1 teaspoon garam masala
- 1 tablespoon sunflower oil
- 1 green chili
- 4 large ripe tomatoes
- 225g paneer
- 1 teaspoon turmeric
- 1 teaspoon ground coriander
- 1 teaspoon ground cumin
- 2.5cm piece ginger

Method:
1. In a deep fryer, flame the oil over medium temperature until it shimmers.
2. Reduce the heat to low and add the paneer.
3. In a sauce, combine the ginger, smoked paprika, turmeric, coriander seeds, chili, and continue cooking.
4. Then use the back of a spoon, mix the tomato in.
5. Stirring occasionally for another two minutes after adding the peas, now stir in the paneer and season with garam masala.
6. Offer with peanut sauce, roti, or rice, divided into two bowls and topped with coriander leaves.

Chapter 7: Indian Desserts Recipes

7.1 Besan Lado Recipe

Cooking Time: 35 minutes
Serving Size: 10 lado

Ingredients:

- ¼ teaspoon cardamom powder
- 2 teaspoons nuts
- ½ cup powdered sugar
- ¼ cup ghee
- 1 cup gram flour

Method:

1. Transfer the ghee to a heavy-bottomed pan and melt it over low pressure.
2. Transfer the poured besan to the pan until the ghee has melted.
3. On medium heat, continue cooking constantly.
4. Switch off the heat in the bowl.
5. Then stir in the cardamom powder.
6. Combine the sugar and peanuts in a mixing bowl.
7. Integrate all of the ingredients in a large mixing bowl before the sugar and nuts are thoroughly mixed.
8. Pinch a little bowl out of the dough now.
9. To make a circular shape, press and roll across your palms.

7.2 Ras Malai Recipe

Cooking Time: 4 hours
Serving Size: 8

Ingredients:

For Rabri

- 5 almonds
- 10 cashews
- 2 tablespoon saffron milk
- 7 pistachios
- 1-liter milk
- ½ teaspoon cardamom powder
- ¼ cup sugar

For Chenna

- 2 tablespoon lemon juice
- 1 cup water
- 1-liter milk

For Sugar Syrup

- 8 cups water
- 1½ cup sugar

Method:

1. To begin, heat the milk.
2. In particular, stir in the lemon juice.
3. Drain and pinch the curdled milk to remove any extra water.
4. Start kneading after thirty minutes.
5. Also, make little balls and flatten them.
6. To begin, combine water and sugar.
7. Get the syrup to a boil for ten minutes.
8. Afterward, release the paneer balls that have been packed.
9. Cook for fifteen minutes with the lid on.
10. Get the milk to a boil.

11.	Glucose, coriander powder, and saffron milk are also added.
12.	Put it in the fridge for another 2-3 hours.
13.	Place the chilled rabri over the balls now.
14.	Finally, add a few nuts as a finishing touch.

7.3 Kaju Katli Recipe

Cooking Time: 25 minutes
Serving Size: 20 piece
Ingredients:
- 1 teaspoon ghee
- Edible silver leaves
- ¼ cup water
- ½ teaspoon rose water
- ½ cup white sugar
- 1 cup cashews

Method:
1. In a seasoning grinder, ground the cashews.
2. To make a smooth powder, combine all ingredients in a blender and blend until smooth.
3. In a medium-sized saucepan, combine the sugar and water.
4. Allow the sugar to dissolve and the mixture to boil for 1 minute.
5. On low pressure, keep swirling the combination.
6. Stir in one teaspoon of ghee.
7. Stir constantly; the dough will quit the pan's edges after about ten minutes on medium heat.
8. Move the flour to a piece of parchment paper until it is done.
9. So, with your fingertips, knead the dough until it is soft.
10.	By slicing the dough horizontally and then vertically, you will make a diamond shape.

11.   Remove the Kaju katli and serve.

7.4 Boondi Lado Recipe

Cooking Time: 40 minutes
Serving Size: 12

Ingredients:
For Boondi

- ¼ teaspoon baking soda
- Oil for deep frying
- 3 drops yellow color
- ¼ cup
- 1 cup gram flour

Other Ingredients

- 5 cloves
- ¼ teaspoon cardamom powder
- 2 tablespoon kishmish
- 2 tablespoon cashew
- 1 tablespoon butter

For Sugar Syrup

- ½ cup water
- 1¼ cup sugar

Method:

1. To begin, make boondi with besan batter.
2. Take 1 ¼ cup of sugar and place it in a big thick-bottomed wok.
3. Place the sugar over the boondi until it has cooled somewhat.
4. Insert one tablespoon olive oil is also used to roast two tablespoon pecans, two tablespoon cashews, and five garlic.
5. Place the roasted dried fruits and ¼ teaspoon coriander powder over the boondi combination.

6. Start preparing ladoo when the combination is still soft.
7. When cold, store in an airtight bag.

7.5 Kheer Recipe

Cooking Time: 45 minutes
Serving Size: 5

Ingredients:
- 3 tablespoons nuts
- 1.5 teaspoons rose water
- 1-liter whole milk
- 5 tablespoons sugar
- ¼ cup rice 50 grams
- 4 green cardamom pods
- 1 teaspoon ghee

Method:
1. Wash the rice until it is completely clean.
2. On moderate fire, heat a heavy-bottomed skillet. Insert one teaspoon peanut oil and 3-4 broken green coriander seeds after that.
3. Then pour in the milk and stir thoroughly.
4. Get the dairy to a boil, which should take between 10-12 minutes.
5. Reduce the heat to low and simmer the kheer for about 25 minutes on medium heat until the milk has risen to a boil.
6. Toss in the sugar and stir to combine. Insert the nuts as well.
7. On incorporating the sugar and almonds, boil the kheer for another five minutes.
8. Remove the pan from the oven, let it cool, and then serve.

7.6 Falooda Recipe

Cooking Time: 30 minutes
Serving Size: 2

Ingredients:

- ½ cup falooda sev
- 5 sliced almonds
- 50-gram sugar
- 4 tablespoon rose syrup
- 5 sliced pistachios
- 2 sliced cherry
- 2 cup milk
- 1 teaspoon falooda
- 4 tablespoon strawberry jelly

Method:

1. In a heavy pan over medium heat, bring the cream and butter to a boil.
2. Pour the rose syrup into the milk thoroughly.
3. Break the jelly in the meantime.
4. Bring a saucepan full of water to a boil over medium-high heat.
5. It will soften if you add falooda sev to it.
6. Enable the falooda seeds to grow in a tiny bowl of water.
7. Pick the cooled serving cups and add rose syrup into each one after a while.
8. After that, add raspberry jelly and flourished falooda beans.
9. Cover them with falooda sev after that.
10. Press the cooled rose milk gradually.
11. Finally, pour some more rose syrup on top. Serve right away.

7.7 Fruit Custard Recipe

Cooking Time: 25 minutes
Serving Size: 5

Ingredients:
- Pinch cardamom powder
- 2 cups assorted fruits
- 3 tablespoons custard powder
- Splash of rose water
- 4-5 tablespoons sugar
- 3 cups whole milk

Method:
1. In a thick bottomed pan over medium-high heat, pour 3 cups milk.
2. Three tablespoons of milk should be removed from the pan and placed in a small cup.
3. Add in 3 teaspoons of custard powder with the cream.
4. Then reduce the heat to low and stir in the sugar until it is well mixed.
5. Begin to incorporate the custard blend.
6. Cook for a further 2-3 minutes, just until the custard has thickened.
7. At about the same moment, chop and chill all of the fruits you will be using in the custard.
8. Shift the custard to a mixing bowl and stir in the fruits after they have chilled.

Chapter 8: Indian Soups Dishes

8.1 Cream of Mushroom Soup

Cooking Time: 50 minutes
Serving Size: 6

Ingredients:

- 1 cup half-and-half
- 1 tablespoon sherry
- ¼ teaspoon salt
- ¼ teaspoon ground black pepper
- 5 cups mushrooms
- 3 tablespoons butter
- 3 tablespoons all-purpose flour
- 1 ½ cups chicken broth
- ⅛ teaspoon dried thyme
- ½ cup chopped onion

Method:

1. Heat mushrooms in liquid with onions and tarragon in a big heavy frying pan before soft, around ten to twenty minutes.
2. Sautee the paste in a food processor or blender, keeping some vegetable chunks in there. Remove from the blender.
3. Heat the oil in a frying pan and stir in the flour until clear.
4. Combine the salt, powder, half-and-half, and food puree in a mixing bowl.
5. Get the soup to a boil, stirring continuously, and prepare until it thickens.
6. Season with salt and pepper to taste, then pour in the sherry.

8.2 Tomato Soup Recipe

Cooking Time: 1 hour and 45 minutes
Serving Size: 6

Ingredients:

- 2 bay leaves
- 1.2 liters hot vegetable stock
- 2 squirts of tomato purée
- A good pinch of sugar
- 1-1.25 kg ripe tomatoes
- 1 celery stick
- 2 tablespoon olive oil
- 1 small carrot
- 1 medium onion

Method:

1. First, have your veggies together.
2. Heat 2 tablespoons olive oil in a big heavy-bottomed pan over medium heat.
3. Then add the onion, cabbage, and fennel and combine with a rolling pin.
4. Put two bay leaves, torn into small pieces, into the bowl.
5. Stir to combine the ingredients, cover the grill, and cook the tomatoes for ten minutes over medium heat.
6. Cook for 30 minutes on low heat, stirring occasionally.
7. Switch off the heat in the pan. Fill your blender halfway with broth.
8. Blitz until the soup is creamy, then transfer to a big mixing cup.

8.3 Palak Soup

Cooking Time: 15 minutes
Serving Size: 2

Ingredients:

- 1 tablespoon cornflour
- 1 teaspoon fresh cream
- ½ teaspoon pepper
- ½ teaspoon sugar
- 1 tablespoon butter
- ½ cup milk
- Salt to taste
- 1 tej patta
- 1 bunch palak
- ¼ cup water
- 1 clove garlic
- ¼ onion

Method:

1. Add the butter and tej leaves to a big wok.
2. Sauté until it begins to smell floral.
3. Add coarsely diced garlic and onions as well.
4. Cook until they are golden brown.
5. Palak leaves should also be added.
6. Sauté for a moment on medium heat, or until they have shrunk in bulk.
7. Mix the combination until it forms a smoother puree, adding more water if needed.
8. Allow the puree to come to a boil.
9. Insert the cornflour mixture and whisk briefly.
10. To create corn flour powder, combine one tablespoon rice flour and ¼ cup water in a mixing bowl.
11. Check the quality by stirring once more.
12. Then, in a serving cup, drain the soup and finish with fresh milk.

8.4 Easy One-Pot Corn Soup

Cooking Time: 30 minutes
Serving Size: 6

Ingredients:
- 5 eggs large, beaten
- 1 teaspoon sesame oil
- 5 tablespoon green onions
- ¼ cup cornstarch
- 1 can corn
- 1 can creamed corn
- 1 tablespoon soy sauce
- 1 cup carrots
- 7 cups chicken broth
- Pepper to taste
- 1 tablespoon sriracha sauce
- 2.5 cups chicken
- 1-2 teaspoon ginger powder
- Salt to taste
- 1-2 teaspoon garlic powder

Method:
1. Take broth, grilled chicken, ginger, garlic, salt, spice, Sriracha sauce, sesame oil, vegetables, corn, cheesed corn, and two tablespoons of fresh basil boil over a moderate flame in a big nonstick pan.
2. Reduce the heat to medium-low and cook for another 8-10 minutes, just until the carrots are tender.
3. Mix with the diluted cornstarch slurry. The broth will thicken as it cooks.
4. Slowly pour in the beaten eggs, stirring gently to create fried egg ribbons.

5. Mix with the remaining three tablespoons, spring onions, and sesame oil.
6. Switch off the heat and serve right away.

8.5 Creamy Bottle Gourd Soup

Cooking Time: 20 minutes
Serving Size: 3

Ingredients:
- Salt and black pepper
- Cilantro
- 1 medium onion
- 1.5 cups water
- 1 medium bottle gourd
- 3 medium garlic cloves
- 1 green chili
- 1 teaspoon olive oil

Method:
1. In the Instant Pot, choose to sauté mode.
2. When the olive oil is sweet, add the minced garlic, vegetables, and green chilies and cook until the onions are softened.
3. Combine the diced bottle gourd, liquid or veggie broth, and salt in a large mixing bowl.
4. Set the timer for five minutes and the container to manual.
5. Allow the pressure to escape as the instant port buzzes spontaneously.
6. Then use a stand mixer, puree the soup until it is almost creamy.
7. Season with black pepper, ground.
8. If desired, garnish with cilantro just before eating.

8.6 Roasted Tomato Soup

Cooking Time: 50 minutes
Serving Size: 6

Ingredients:
- ½ cup basil leaves
- ¾ cup heavy cream
- 2 bay leaves
- 4 tablespoons butter
- 2 ½ pounds fresh tomatoes
- Salt and black pepper
- 1-quart chicken stock
- 6 cloves garlic
- Vine cherry tomatoes
- ½ cup extra-virgin olive oil
- 2 small yellow onions

Method:
1. Preheat the oven to 450 degrees Fahrenheit.
2. Tomatoes should be washed, cored, and sliced in half.
3. On a baking tray, arrange the tomatoes, peppercorns, and vegetables.
4. Sprinkle with salt and drizzle with ½ cup olive oil.
5. Switch the diced peppers, onion, and garlic to a big stockpot from the stove.
6. ¾ chicken stock, garlic cloves, and butter are added.
7. If using, wipe down basil leaves before adding them to the bowl.
8. Erase the bay leaves before pureeing the soup with an electric mixer until creamy.
9. Sprinkle with salt and ground black pepper to satisfy.

10.   Three or four roasted grape sun-dried tomatoes and a dash of heavy cream can be garnished in the dish.

8.7 Carrot Tomato Soup

Cooking Time: 1 hour and 15 minutes
Serving Size: 8

Ingredients:

- 1 tablespoon red wine vinegar
- 250ml whole milk
- 2 vegetable stock cubes
- 1 tablespoon sugar
- 3 tablespoon olive oil
- 500g carton passata
- 750g cherry tomato
- 2 onions
- 250g floury potato
- 5 bay leaves
- 1¼ kg carrot
- 2 celery sticks

Method:

1. In your biggest frying pan, softly steam the oil, onion, and fennel until cooled.
2. For several minutes, add the potatoes and carrots, and add all of the rest of the ingredients, except the milk, along with 1-liter water.
3. Take to a low boil, then reduce to low heat.
4. Cover and cook for thirty minutes, then open and continue to cook for another thirty minutes.
5. Remove the basil leaves and mix the broth with a hand blender until smooth.

6. Pour in the milk or as much water as necessary.
7. Adjust with salt and pepper to taste, then warm through it and eat with the crispy hot cross buns.

8.8 Cream of Broccoli Soup

Cooking Time: 35 minutes
Serving Size: 6
Ingredients:
- 2 cups milk
- Ground black pepper
- 8 cups broccoli florets
- 3 tablespoons all-purpose flour
- 5 tablespoons butter
- 1 stalk celery
- 3 cups chicken broth
- 1 onion

Method:
1. A moderate, slow cooker, melt two tablespoons of butter and sauté tomato and fennel until soft.
2. Cover and cook for an additional with the broccoli and broth.
3. In a mixer, puree the broth. Blend in batches until light and fluffy, then transfer to a clean pot.
4. Peel 3 tablespoons butter in a small saucepan, then stir in flour and dairy.
5. Stir once thick, then bubbly, and transfer to the broth.
6. Serve with a pinch of black pepper.

Chapter 9: Indian Salad Recipes

9.1 Bean Sprouts and Salad Recipe

Cooking Time: 12 minutes
Serving Size: 2

Ingredients:

- 1 green onion
- 9 oz. bean sprouts

Seasonings

- ½ tablespoon soy sauce
- ¼ teaspoon kosher/sea salt
- 1 clove garlic
- 1 tablespoon sesame oil
- 1 tablespoon white sesame seeds

Method:

1. Dump the bean sprouts thoroughly after rinsing them in cold water.
2. A huge pot of water should be brought to a boil.
3. Once the water has come to a boil, add the bean sprouts and simmer for 2 - 5 minutes.
4. Drain and set it aside for five minutes in a saucepan.
5. Break the spring onions into small bits in the meantime.
6. In a pestle and mortar, ground the caraway seeds.
7. Grate or grind the garlic cloves with a garlic press.
8. Combine all of the spice components in a medium mixing bowl and stir well.
9. In a large mixing cup, add the bean sprouts and spring onions.

10.   Freeze or serve at ambient temperature.

9.2 Broccoli and Baby Corn Salad

Cooking Time: 15 minutes
Serving Size: 6
Ingredients:
Salad Ingredients
- 1 large carrot grated
- ¼ cup cranberries
- 1 cup cherry tomatoes
- ½ can produce corn or corn
- 2 medium broccoli

Dressing Ingredients
- 4 tablespoon mayo
- 1 large garlic clove
- 4 tablespoon ranch

Method:
1. Broccoli should be chopped into small thin strips.
2. Merge sliced broccoli, two tablespoons sliced tomatoes, corn cobs, one red onion, and ¼ cup blueberries in a large mixing bowl.
3. Combine four tablespoon ranch dressing, four tablespoon mayonnaise, and 2 pressed garlic powder in a shallow mixing bowl or measuring cup.
4. Toss the salad with the dressing and adjust the seasonings to taste.

9.3 Rajma Salad

Cooking Time: 40 minutes

Serving Size: 4

> **Ingredients:**
> - Mint leaves
> - Salt, to taste
> - 1 teaspoon chaat masala powder
> - 1 lemon, juiced
> - 2 cups rajma
> - 1 tomato
> - 2 green chilies
> - 1 onion

Method:

1. Soak the rajma overtime and pressure bake for four to six whistles with water.
2. Reduce the heat to low and continue to cook for the next 20 minutes after four to six whistles.
3. Enable the pressure to dissipate normally. Rajma must be roasted and soft.
4. Drain the accumulated water and set aside the rajma if there is any.
5. Add the chopped rajma, carrots, peppers, green chile sauce, chaat masala paste, salt, fresh mint, and lime juice to a mixing cup.
6. Toss the rajma salad together thoroughly.
7. Taste for salt and change as needed. Chill before serving.

9.4 Paneer and Chana Salad

Cooking Time: 30 minutes
Serving Size: 3

> **Ingredients:**
> - 1 tablespoon lime juice
> - 1 teaspoon virgin olive oil

- 1 green chili
- Salt as required
- 1 cup soaked chickpeas
- ½ cup cubed paneer
- 1 tomato
- 4 leaves spinach
- 1 handful coriander leaves
- black pepper
- 1 onion
- ½ teaspoon chaat masala powder
- 1 handful black olives

Method:

1. To make this tasty salad, drench the chickpeas overnight and cook them until tender.
2. Slice the cabbage, green chilies, and onion in the meantime.
3. Merge the paneer balls, chickpeas, and sliced veggies in a big mixing cup.
4. Add the green olives and cut the basil leaf.
5. To make the dressing, whisk together the canola oil, chaat masala paste, lime juice, and spice powder in a mixing cup.
6. Toss the salad in this sauce thoroughly. Serve with cilantro as a garnish.

9.5 Healthy Lunch Salad

Cooking Time: 20 minutes
Serving Size: 6

Ingredients:

- 1 large ripe avocado
- ½ tablespoon mixed sesame seeds

- ½ cucumber
- 3 spring onions
- 250g sirloin steaks
- 12 radishes
- 3 carrots
- Thumb-sized piece ginger
- 3 red bird's eye chilies
- 4 lettuces
- 2 tablespoon sesame oil
- 1 tablespoon low-salt soy sauce
- 2 limes, juiced
- 1 garlic clove

Method:

1. Prepare the salad dressing by stirring together all the garlic, ginger, lemon zest, oil, oil, and minced chilies in a cup just before frying.
2. Place the steaks on the grill and bake for three minutes on the one hand, then change and grill for another three minutes for medium-rare.
3. Wrap and set aside the meat for five minutes after it has finished cooking.
4. On a shared tray, place the salad leaves, radishes, cabbage, grapefruit, green onions, and avocado.
5. Cut the steak thinly against the grains and serve on top of the lettuce.
6. Drizzle any remaining juices and seasoning over the top.
7. Serve with sesame oil and cut red chili as a garnish.

9.6 Bean Sprout and Macaroni Salad

Cooking Time: 30 minutes

Serving Size: 8

Ingredients:

Soy-Ginger Dressing

- 2 tablespoons mayonnaise
- ¼ cup vegetable oil
- 1 teaspoon ground ginger
- ¾ teaspoon pepper flakes
- 1 tablespoon sugar
- 1 tablespoon sesame oil
- 6 tablespoons soy sauce
- 1 tablespoon rice wine vinegar
- 3 medium garlic

Pasta Salad

- ½ cup peanuts
- ¼ cup cilantro
- 2 cups bean sprouts
- 3 green onions
- 3 medium carrots
- 1 medium red bell pepper
- 2 tablespoons salt
- 8 ounces broccoli florets
- 1 pound beef
- 1 pound penne pasta

Method:

1. In a 2-cup Pyrex mason jar, combine the garlic, sesame oil, salt, starch, soy sauce, spice, and pepper seasoning.
2. Mix in the tomato sauce until dry, then drizzle in the oil in a long, steady stream to create an emulsions dressing; chill until prepared to use.
3. In a big soup pot, bring 1 liter of water and two teaspoons of salt to a simmer.

4. Insert the spaghetti and cook until only tender, whisking frequently and incorporating the broccoli over the last moment.
5. Set aside as you finish cooking the rest of the salad ingredients.
6. Combine all salad ingredients in a big mixing bowl or a gallon-size zip pack.
7. When ready to eat, insert the dressing and toss it to cover.

9.7 Peas and Potato Salad

Cooking Time: 45 minutes
Serving Size: 6

Ingredients:

- ½ teaspoon salt
- ¼ cup red onion
- 1 tablespoon apple cider vinegar
- 1 teaspoon dried tarragon
- 2 lbs. red potatoes
- ¾ cup mayonnaise
- 1 tablespoon Dijon mustard
- ½ cup frozen peas

Method:

1. Get a pan of salted water to a boil with the potatoes.
2. Reduce heat to low and continue to cook until the vegetables are tender.
3. Add peas for two minutes until the potatoes are finished.
4. Drain the water and set it aside to cool to ambient temperature.
5. Potatoes can be cut into wedges.

6. Merge mayonnaise, vinegar, mustard, thyme, and salt in a big mixing cup.
7. Toss in the potatoes, beans, and sliced onion until it is evenly covered.
8. Refrigerate for 1 hour until it is ready to use.

9.8 Cabbage and Grape Salad

Cooking Time: 35 minutes
Serving Size: 4

Ingredients:
- ¼ cup sunflower seeds
- 2 tablespoons chives
- ½ small red cabbage
- 1½ cups seedless grapes
- 2 tablespoons red wine vinegar
- Kosher salt and pepper
- ¼ cup olive oil
- 1 teaspoon dijon mustard
- ½ teaspoon thyme
- ½ teaspoons sugar

Method:
1. In a big mixing cup, combine red wine vinegar, salt, cayenne pepper, minced chives, kosher salt, and a few squeezes of pepper.
2. Add the olive oil and whisk to combine.
3. Combine sliced red cabbage, doubled seedless grapes, pickled roasted seeds, and sliced chives in a shallow mixing bowl.
4. Season with salt and pepper.
5. Allow for at least a few minutes of resting time before serving.

Chapter 10: Most Famous Indian Dishes

10.1 Rajma Chawal

Cooking Time: 45 minutes
Serving Size: 4

Ingredients:

- 1 tablespoon black pepper
- 1 tablespoon ghee
- 1 tablespoon garam masala powder
- 1 black cardamom
- 1 cup red kidney beans
- 1 tablespoon cumin powder
- Salt as required
- 1 tablespoon garlic
- 2 chopped green chili
- 2 large tomato
- 1 cup rice
- 2 clove
- 3 tablespoon mustard oil
- 2 large onion
- 1 cinnamon stick
- 2 green cardamom
- 1 teaspoon ginger
- 1 tablespoon black pepper
- 1 tablespoon coriander powder

Method:

1. Rajma should be washed.

2. Pressure cook with 2 cups sugar, one tablespoon salt, and turmeric.
3. Finely cut the onions and set them aside, as well as the tomatoes, which should be grated and set aside.
4. Get a spice, onion, and sweet chili paste.
5. Add mustard oil to a depth skillet.
6. Cook until lightly browned, then add the onions.
7. Heat on medium for 4-5 minutes after adding the tomatoes.
8. Combine the ginger, cloves, and sweet chili sauce, as well as the spices.
9. Cook until the spices are fragrant and the oil begins to run down the sides of the pan.
10. Now insert one cup of hot water and the rajma.
11. Pour the rice into the water.
12. Strain the water until the rice is soft and doubled in size.
13. Enable the rice to cool for 2-3 minutes after spreading it out on a pan.
14. Serve immediately with the Rajma that has been prepared.

10.2 Lucknowi Biryani

Cooking Time: 40 minutes
Serving Size: 6

Ingredients:
- 1 pinch saffron
- 1 large onion
- 3 teaspoon ghee
- 4 tablespoon refined oil
- ½ teaspoon mace powder
- 2 black cardamom

- 1 inches cinnamon stick
- 1 teaspoon fennel seeds
- 1 teaspoon black pepper
- 2 cup basmati rice
- 10 clove
- 2 teaspoon cumin seeds
- 2 teaspoon salt
- 2½ cup milk
- 2 teaspoon coriander seeds
- 3 green cardamom
- ½ kilograms mutton
- 2-star anise

For Marination

- 1 teaspoon red chili powder
- 1 pinch garam masala powder
- 4 teaspoon yogurt
- 1 teaspoon garlic paste
- 1 teaspoon ginger paste
- 2 teaspoon cashews
- 1 teaspoon turmeric

Method:

1. Dry roast all of the whole ingredients to make garam masala. Fold the quantity of water used to boil the rice.
2. Combine the food items for meat marination. Refrigerate it for an hour after covering it with a plate.
3. Finely chop the onion and cook it in a little oil before setting it aside. Salt and pepper the beef. In the handi, combine the peanut oil and the oil. Switch the marinated steak from the container to the handi until it is hot enough.

4. On high heat, stir and simmer the meat for a few seconds. In the meantime, transfer the saffron to the dairy and stir well to unleash the saffron color and scent into the milk. The mutton can now be layered with cooked rice, followed by the saffron cooking liquid.
5. Cover your handiwork. Cook for about 30 minutes and serve.

10.3 Chana Masala

Cooking Time: 35 minutes
Serving Size: 4

Ingredients:

- Lemon wedges
- Fresh cilantro
- 1 large can of tomatoes
- 2 cans chickpeas
- 1 cup basmati rice
- ½ teaspoon turmeric
- Pinch of cayenne pepper
- 2 tablespoons coconut oil
- 1 ½ teaspoons coriander
- ¾ teaspoon cumin
- 1 onion
- 1 tablespoon ginger
- 1 ½ teaspoons garam masala
- ½ teaspoon fine sea salt
- 5 cloves garlic
- 1 serrano

Method:

1. Prepare the rice. Remove the cap and fluff the grain with a spoon, seasoning to taste with kosher salt.
2. Add the oil in a small Dutch oven or big saucepan over medium-low heat.
3. Combine the carrot, chiles, and salt in a mixing bowl.
4. Cook for about five minutes or until the onions are soft.
5. Cook for 30 seconds to 1 minute, till the cloves and spice are fragrant.
6. Cook, stirring continuously, for the next minute after adding the spices.
7. Toss in the tomatoes, along with their juices.
8. Add the lentils and boost the oven temperature.
9. Take the combination to a low boil, then reduce to low heat.
10. If needed, season with more salt to taste.
11. If chosen, pour-over basmati rice with a lemon slice or two and a sprinkling of dried basil leaves.

10.4 Kadhi Chawal

Cooking Time: 55 minutes
Serving Size: 5

Ingredients:
For Kadhi

- 1 chili
- 2 tablespoon coriander
- Pinch asafoetida
- 1 onion
- One teaspoon coriander seeds
- 1 dried red chili

- 1 teaspoon jeera
- ½ teaspoon pepper
- 5 tablespoon gram flour
- 2 tablespoon oil
- ½ teaspoon fenugreek
- 1 cup yogurt
- 5 cup water
- ½ teaspoon turmeric
- ½ tablespoon ginger garlic paste
- 1 teaspoon salt
- ¼ teaspoon carom seeds
- 1 teaspoon red chili powder

For Tempering
- 1 dried red chili
- ½ teaspoon red chili powder
- 1 teaspoon cumin
- 1 tablespoon ghee

Method:
1. First, combine the besan, turmeric, chili powder, ajwain, spice garlic paste, pepper, and curd in a large mixing bowl.
2. Mix thoroughly to create a stable paste.
3. Now add 4 cups of water and stir thoroughly. Set aside for now.
4. Two tablespoons oil, ½ teaspoon methi, one teaspoon smoked paprika, ½ teaspoon salt, one teaspoon cilantro seeds, one red chili, and pinch hing heated in a wide wok.
5. Prepare the pakoras according to the package directions.
6. Pour the pakoras into the kadhi that has been packed.
7. Heat 1 tablespoon ghee to make the tempering.
8. Add two tablespoons coriander to the tempering and spill over the kadhi. Blend well.

9. Finally, serve the kadhi pakora with boiled vegetables or jeera rice.

10.5 Masala Dosa

Cooking Time: 1 hour
Serving Size: 10

Ingredients:
For the Dosa Batter

- ½ teaspoon salt
- Vegetable oil
- One teaspoon fenugreek seeds
- ½ cup urad dal
- 2 cups short-grain rice

For the Potato Filling

- 1 ½ pounds potatoes
- ½ cup cilantro
- 4 garlic cloves, minced
- 2 small green chiles
- 1 tablespoon grated ginger
- 8 curry leaves
- 3 tablespoons ghee
- ½ teaspoon turmeric
- Pinch of asafetida
- 1 teaspoon mustard seeds
- 1 medium onion
- ½ teaspoon salt
- 2 small hot red peppers
- ½ teaspoon cumin seeds

Method:

1. In a pan, clean the rice thoroughly and coat it with 4 cups of ice water.

2. In a small container, combine the urad dal and fenugreek nuts, rinse properly, and cover cold water.
3. In different colanders, drain the rice and the dal-fenugreek combination.
4. Fill a stick blender, mixer, or wet-dry slicer halfway with rice.
5. In a large mixing dish, combine two blends.
6. Add enough water to make a medium-thick mixture by whisking it together.
7. There should be around 6 cups total.
8. In a large skillet, melt ghee over medium-high heat.
9. Toss in the potatoes and half a cup of water.
10. Heat, constantly stirring, for around five minutes, or until the fluid has faded away.
11. Set a broiler pan or cast-iron pan over medium heat to create dosas.
12. ½ teaspoon oil drizzled over the edge.
13. Allow dosa batter to color on one side only until the outer layers start to look clean, about two minutes.
14. Marginally deflate the potato blend. Cook and serve right away.

10.6 Dal Makhani

Cooking Time: 2 hours 10 minutes
Serving Size: 5
Ingredients:
To Pressure Cook
- 1 teaspoon salt
- 3.5 cups water
- ¼ cup rajma
- ¾ cup urad dal

Masala for the Dal

- More Amul butter
- Piece of charcoal
- ½ teaspoon sugar
- ¼ cup cream
- 1 tablespoon ghee
- ½ teaspoon salt or to taste
- 1.5 cups water
- 3 tablespoons butter
- ½ teaspoon red chili powder
- ¼ teaspoon garam masala
- Two teaspoons ginger garlic
- ½ cup tomato puree
- 1 medium white onion

Method:

1. In a big mixing cup, rinse and wash the urad grain and rajma.
2. Add one teaspoon salt to the dal and rajma in a slow cooker.
3. Heat for ten minutes at medium temperature, then reduce to the low-medium pan and stir for another ten minutes.
4. Then use a stick blender, mix some of the dal and rajma.
5. Warm two tablespoons of oil in a pan, in order to make the paratha.
6. Heat for 1 to 2 minutes after adding the spice garlic paste.
7. Toss in the tomato puree and blend well.
8. Add in the dal that has been boiled.

9. Curry paste, red chili paste, and salt are added to the pan.

10.   Stir in ½ cup water and reduce heat to low.

11.   Just after dal has stewed for 45 minutes, add the butter and blend well.

12.   Position the steel bowl on the tops of the trivet and fill it with hot charcoal.

13.   Ghee should be heated and poured on top of the charcoal.

14.   Represent with a tap of Amul oil and more milk on top of the dal makhani.

10.7 Rogan Josh

Cooking Time: 2 hours 20 minutes
Serving Size: 5

Ingredients:

- 1 ½ tablespoon fennel powder
- 1 ¼ tablespoon flour
- 2 pinch saffron
- 1 tablespoon red chili powder
- 1 kilograms mutton
- 4 red chili
- 1 ¼ tablespoon coriander powder
- ½ teaspoon asafoetida
- 1 ¼ teaspoon cumin seeds
- 1 teaspoon peppercorns
- 2 cinnamon
- 2 ½ tablespoon milk
- 150 gm hung curd

* 5 black cardamom
* Salt as required
* ½ cup ghee
* One ¼ teaspoon ginger powder
* 1 ½ cup water

For Garnishing

* Coriander leaves

Method:

1. To make this delicious taste, first, make the saffron dairy by boiling saffron in milk for several hours.
2. Then, in the slow cooker, add entire red chilies, chopped garlic, and asafetida and cook for few seconds.
3. After that, add the meat bits and stir thoroughly.
4. Remove the cap after 5 minutes and add ½ cup of water, stirring well with the seasoning.
5. In the meantime, in a shallow mixing cup, combine all-purpose flour and yogurt, and stir well.
6. In a large mixing bowl, combine all of the spices.
7. Later, in the slow cooker, add 1 cup of water and steam the meat for 1-2 hours on medium.
8. Marinade and serve immediately with chapati or hummus.
9. This recipe can also be served with rice.

Conclusion

India's culinary is one of the most versatile in the world, distinguished by its refined and delicate use of the many herbs, spices, seeds, and fruits produced throughout the country. The diverse populations of the culturally mixed Indian subcontinent are reflected in each geographical region's culinary, including a wide variety of recipes and prepared foods. The spiritual traditions and culture of India have influenced the development of its food. Many Buddhist, Hindu, and Jain cultures follow a vegetarian diet. For its long cultural impact on the continent's food cultures, Indian cuisine is common in Southeast Asia. The middle ages saw the impact of Indian cuisine on traditional Malaysian recipes. Vegetarianism's spread across Asia is mostly attributed to old Hindu Buddhist traditions. When it comes to various spices in Indian cuisine, there are many health benefits. Prepare foods, explore with ingredients, and use these dishes to enjoy a healthier and more enjoyable life.

www.ingramcontent.com/pod-product-compliance
Lightning Source LLC
Chambersburg PA
CBHW061527120726
48001CB00004B/1424